IMPOSE YOUR WILL

OVER YOUR BODY

MARCUS T. TAYLOR

Impose Your Will Over Your Body
All rights reserved © 2016 by Marcus T. Taylor

This novel is a work of fiction. Any resemblances to real people, living or dead, actual events, establishments, organizations, or locales are intended to give the fiction a sense of reality. Other names, characters, places, and incidents are either products of the author's imagination or are used fictitiously.

ISBN:0999018701

LCCN: TBD

Editing and Typesetting: 21st Street Urban Editing
21StreetUrbanEditing.com

Cover Design: Tommie Hayes-Fonder, Designer
Grafik House Designs and Solutions
North Chicago, Illinois
TheGrafikHouse@gmail.com

WILL

I do not know what I am doing.[a]

For what I want to do, I do not do, but what I hate, I do. What a wretched man I am! Who will rescue me from this body of death?[b]

CONTEXT

꙰

This book does not have to be read from front to back...

ADDICTION

ৎ৽৾ঌ

If I weren't under the influence of alcohol, I would have made better choices for myself. Sadly, enough, that wasn't the case. My alcohol consumption was off the chain. I never had the desire to quit drinking, but I did desire to control it. The more I tried to get my drinking under control, the more it controlled me. I tried everything to quit drinking. I tried to put a limit on it. I tried to drink only beer. I tried drinking only on the weekends or only at night. Nothing I did seemed to work. All I ended up doing was pretending I was handling my alcohol better and that didn't work well either. I remember having a conversation with my grandfather and out of the blue, he told me that I needed to stop drinking. Automatically I got defensive.

"I don't drink no more…"

"…And no less either," he replied.

I mean really, who was I kidding? I couldn't control my drinking. I had an alcohol problem and combined with that, I had a pack of cigarettes a day smoking habit. This led me to questioning myself. *What is in alcohol that causes it to have so much control over me? Grapes and corn? What's in cigarettes? Nicotine and tobacco?*

Here I was, supposed to be the head of my household-the king of my castle, and yet fruits and plants were controlling me. What kind of king was I? Why can't I participate or be a part of anything without drinking? Why can't I enjoy watching a ball game without a case of beer? Why couldn't I go to a cookout without returning back home inebriated? Why did I continue to drink until I passed out, only to wake up hours later feeling miserable? Why smoke when I can't stand the way cigarettes make me, and everything around me, smell badly? Why do I smoke knowing it is harmful to my lungs? Why, when it turns my teeth and nails yellow? I'm exhausted all the time and it causes me to wheeze, cough, and hack up phlegm thick enough to chew on. Yuck!

I spent years without an answer to any of my questions about my alcohol and nicotine addiction. I've always admired people who could have an occasional cigar at a graduation or welcoming a newborn baby into their family. People who could drink socially, and stop before they become drunk. The next day they're right back to business as usual. How could these people enjoy a night without smoking and drinking, and I couldn't? Moreover, they seemed to stop with little to no effort while on the other hand, I couldn't stop drinking and smoking if my life depended on it. Which it did.

The more I smoked and drank, the more I questioned myself. I hated being drunk. I use to ask myself if I could live without drinking. My answer to myself: *Why would I want to?* I felt that there was nothing wrong with drinking as long as I had control over it. So I spent years trying to control my drinking without any success. One day, I opened my eyes and realized the truth: I had no control. I was trying to do the impossible because no one can control alcohol, nicotine or any other drug for that matter. Alcohol, like any other drug, is going to do what it is meant to do. My best bet was to get better authority over myself.

I began to realize that I didn't have an alcohol problem. My problem was that I blamed everything on alcohol. What I had was a problem with myself. I had no control over my life. A better question to ask myself was, *What is my problem? What's causing me to desire alcohol all the time?* Once I looked beyond the surface, pain stood out as the motivating factor behind my drinking.

I used alcohol to numb my pain. You see, pain is what causes people to lay in bed all day high off prescription medications. Pain is what causes people to be belligerent drunks. Pain is what causes people to smoke marijuana until they're stuck in a stupor, laughing hysterically. Pain is what causes people to lose their jobs, sell all of their possessions, and become thieves and prostitute their bodies for crack. Pain is what keeps you up for five days straight, geeking off meth. Pain is the reason people will chase the heroin that could potentially turn off their lights. Pain is what keeps people doing drugs and alcohol at the expense of their health, families and careers. People will risk destroying their lives and others to alleviate the pain. I personally practiced getting drunk as a teenager because I thought that was what grown men did. Along the way, I discovered that alcohol was a magical substance that numbed the pain and made me feel better about myself. While alcohol helped me ease the pain, it was not the cure. Like most medication, alcohol requires that you use the drug all the time to lessen the pain. Over time, you build a tolerance that requires a higher dosage to be able to deal with your discomfort. I didn't need some temporary alleviation. What I needed most was a cure. What began as me trying to get an innocent chimpanzee off my back, quickly spiraled into me fighting a vicious gorilla. Those of us who have addictions always try to break them.

Sometimes we partake in success only to be returned back to failures. We struggle to figure out *why* we have the addiction to begin with, but before we can get the monkey off of our backs, we must first figure out why it is there to begin with.

I had to go back to the very beginning for me to understand what made the monkey jump on my back to begin with. I was brought up in a loving home with my mother, sister and stepfather, who was actually my sister's biological father, and whom I called dad. My stepfather raised me from the time I was two years old and was my hero and role model. I loved him dearly growing up, and he always spent quality time with me. When I was barely able to walk, he would pull me all around town in a little red wagon. As soon as I was able to ride my bike without training wheels, he took me bike riding. We always played catch together and I don't think we went anywhere without a baseball and gloves in the trunk. Every time it snowed, I could count on my dad to take my sister and I sledding until our hands and feet were frozen. When it came to toys, my dad bought me everything a child could ever want. He bought me all the latest video games; my first BB gun and even a weight bench so I could become strong like him.

Hands down, I had the best dad in the world. There wasn't anything he couldn't fix or build and I enjoyed being his apprentice. I was my dad's pride and joy and everyone knew it by the way he bragged on me. I admired him because he knew how to make up for his mess-ups. I remember a time he had forgotten to leave me money for a school field trip. The school called my dad at work to pick me up because I wasn't able to attend the field trip with my class. My dad not only picked me up, he took the rest of the day off work so he could spend the day at the movies with me.

Spending quality time with my dad was better than any school trip I ever went on.

As a child, I was very small for my age. On top of that, I started school early which made me a year behind the rest of my class. Despite my size, I was the best at everything. Often while drinking beers with his friends, my dad would get into an argument about whose son will whip who in a fight, who could jump the highest or run the fastest and the list goes on and on. It's safe to say, I never disappointed him. I always did exactly what he said I would do. I always came in first in every physical competition and I always made honor roll worthy grades in school. All I wanted to ever be was just like my dad.

My dad had a problem with alcohol and drugs. I had to deal with my mom and dad arguing all the time due to his drinking. Sometimes, my dad wouldn't even make it home by bedtime. When he did decide to stumble in the house in the middle of the night, my sister and I wouldn't be able to go back to sleep from all the racket he and my mother made from arguing and fighting all night. Eventually, he started a family elsewhere and stopped coming home altogether. This tore my family apart. We all were praying for him to come back home and in-between time, my mother became very depressed and isolated herself to her bedroom away from my sister and I. My sister became sad and would often cry out for her daddy, while I felt lost and abandoned. Not only did I lose my stepfather, I lost my stepfather's side of the family. My grandparents, aunties and uncles that I grew up loving had disappeared from my life. I remember whenever my dad used to leave the house he would always tell me, "While I'm gone, you are the man of the house so take care of it." When I finally came to terms with my dad not coming back home, I knew I was permanently the man of the house. My mother no longer had money for me to do any extracurricular activities and she often complained about how far behind she was on bills. After seeing how hard my mother was struggling trying to raise two kids on her own, all I wanted to do was please her and make her happy.

Early on I made up my mind to do what I could to help out, as the man of the house should. At eleven years old, I got my first job as a caddy and it paid extremely well. There were weeks in the summer that I made over six hundred dollars which was pretty good money for an eleven-year-old. I was very proud of myself and I took a lot of the load off of my mother's shoulder. I no longer randomly asked her for money. I bought my own school clothes and helped with my sisters. I even helped out with some of the bills. I kept my grades up in school and I was a star football player. I expected my mother to commend or give me some sort of recognition for how great of a man I was, but it never came. Nevertheless, my mother finally came up out of her depression stage and started dating. It was very apparent that my mother's boyfriends didn't care for me, nor my sister. They just wanted to be with my mother. I spent a lot of time comparing my mothers' boyfriends to my stepfather… none could come close to measuring up.

My mother eventually started seeing my biological father and he became a part of our family. He wasn't anything like my dad, but overtime I grew attached to him. He showed concern and spent time with me. He showed up to all my basketball and football games eventually becoming the head coach of my team. We spent much of our time on a fishing bank, which I enjoyed. My biological father was very different from my "dad". He was very empathetic and forgiving were as my step dad wasn't. I could talk to him about any and everything without judgment. We had become very close, or so I thought.

One summer he and my mother dropped me and my sister off down south for our summer vacation. When I returned home, I found out that my parents had split up and my biological father had moved more than six hundred miles away. I felt abandoned all over again. Every father figure that I have ever had, left without keeping in touch with me. They just turned their backs and walked off. I brushed it off and moved on with my life with the attitude of not needing or wanting a father and headed into my teenage years. Besides, what did I need a father for when I had my mother?

I was a 4' 10" and a 97 pound, freshmen playing football my high school freshman year. I learned that I was no longer the fastest or the strongest and that I was dramatically undersized but, I was still a pretty good football player. One day our freshmen team was scrimmaging with the sophomores and I tackled this kid who was twice my size and severely sprained my back while doing it. My pride would not allow me to tell the coach, instead I just walked off the field and never returned. The next day I woke up with my back as stiff as a board. I informed my mother on how bad my back was hurting and she told me to put some Icy-Hot on it. Given that it took me nearly twenty minutes to put on my socks, I knew putting Icy-Hot on my back would never happen. I didn't need any Icy-Hot anyway. What I needed was a doctor. I walked around home and school for a couple of months suffering from excruciating back pain and no one even noticed.

My mother, who use to show up to all of my football games, never even bothered to ask me how football or school was going. It didn't take long for me to feel neglected and that no one cared about me. The only time my mother spoke to me was when she was fussing about something. Me and my little sister, who was actually bigger than me, argued about everything. My mom's new found boyfriend never had anything to say to me except for when he was trying to boss me around. My loving home that I vowed to take care of and felt the most comfortable at, all of a sudden made me feel like an outcast. Within no time, my teachers were letting my mother know how I was doing by sending conduct reports home every day and my grades in school plummeted. I had begun to spend all of my time in the streets. The streets gave me attention and showed me love so I dropped out of school, left my mother's home and put my heart into the streets. I sold crack and marijuana to provide for myself. I smoked cigarettes and drank alcohol to feel grown and pass time. Just as fast as I left my mother's home, I returned on juvenile house arrest for selling cocaine to an undercover cop. I didn't need anyone to tell me, I messed up, I knew I had.

At the age of fourteen, there I was trying to get my life back together. I went back to school and I even lucked up and got a job working at a local grocery store. I loved my job. My boss showed me respect and treated me like he did every other employee. He made me feel like a young man versus the fourteen-year-old boy that I was. At school and at home, it was a different story. My school schedule was overloaded to help me make up for the time I had missed so I could graduate on time. It was difficult playing catch up and I didn't want any parts of it. I hated school. Being forced to take on extra classes only made matters worse. At school, I felt out of place and inferior to all of my peers. I was probably the only sophomore in the world who was still losing baby teeth. All I wanted to do was turn sixteen and get my G.E.D. My mother and probation officer demanded that I stay in school. When report cards came around, my mother saw that I had an *F* in English. She blamed me working for the bad grade and told me to quit my job. I refused to quit and my mother dragged me right to my boss's office and said, "My son can't work here anymore because he has bad grades in school."

Had I known she was going to do that, I would have rather just not shown up again. It was humiliating sitting next to my mother in front of my boss, the man who taught me how to tie my first tie, and be treated like a child. I felt so low and abysmal. I couldn't believe that my mother embarrassed me like that.

Periodically, I had to go in front of the judge to determine whether I was complying with house arrest or not. If he agreed that I wasn't complying, it was possible that he could revoke my house arrest and have me locked up until I turned eighteen. My lawyer enlightened the judge to all of the good things I was doing. When the judge asked my mother how I was doing, she contradicted everything my lawyer told the judge. My mother told the judge that I didn't listen to her, that I always argued with my sister and that I was getting bad grades in school. She even told him that I didn't take out the trash when I was supposed to. After hearing from my mother, the judge ordered that I be remanded to custody. My lawyer was just as shocked as I was. I did about two weeks in jail before the judge let me back out on house arrest. I was ordered to comply with all of the rules. It was ordered that I stay at home twenty-four hours a day unless I was with my mother or at school. One day my older cousin came by to check up on me. We talked in the kitchen for a minute and then we went to have a smoke on the back porch. My mother reminded me that I wasn't allowed to go on the back porch, but I went anyway. When I came back in the house, I found my mother on the phone with my house arrest officer, informing them that I had left the house. I couldn't believe my eyes and ears. I couldn't believe my mother had betrayed me. The consequences for me leaving out of the house would mean jail until I became an adult. I could not believe that she would risk her son being in jail until he turned eighteen. The son who consoled her in his arms after every time she got into a fight with dad. The same son who at ten years old, rode his bike to the doctor to get an immunization shot all by himself to prevent her from taking off work. The same thoughtful son who went around the house and wrapped up household items as gifts so she wouldn't be without Christmas presents. My heart was broken. Both of my dads abandoned me and all I had was my mother who was now against me. I decided to gather up my belongings and leave. There was no chance I was going to let them lock me up. Besides that, there was no way I was going to live with someone who wanted me in jail.

From that point on, my life took a turn for the worse. I spent nearly the next fifteen years of my life drunk, in and out of jail, being an unproductive citizen, father, and son. I was very unreliable and irresponsible and I couldn't be depended on. I didn't care much about myself and lacked drive and motivation. All I wanted to do was drink. Before I knew it, I fell deep into the bottle. I was suffering from a broken heart that desperately needed to be mended. Alcohol was how I coped with all of my problems. Alcohol kept me content and relaxed while at the same time, being absent minded to any of my responsibilities. I was a functional drunk who could walk, talk, laugh and play but I couldn't take care of any of my obligation. I was now an adult with children who literally had nothing going for myself. I was a nobody who would use girls for sex to stop from feeling worthless. I would seduce girls that I normally wouldn't give the time of day just to feel superior. Occasionally, I would wake up sober and realize the big hole I dug for myself and decide to make an attempt to climb out. I expected different results, but continued to get the same because I continued to do the same things. I didn't need anyone to tell me that I was a big loser, or bum because it was obvious. Every time I got a sense of failure I turned to the bottle because it dulled my conscience and made me forget about everything that mattered.

I hung out with nothing but losers that the only thing I had in common with was the thirst for booze. Our idea of a good time was getting each other sloppy drunk then telling each other how ignorant and stupid we were the night before. I got so accustomed to this type of lifestyle that I thought a house full of drunk people was considered a party. I never wanted to go to any type of festivity or social gathering if alcohol wasn't allowed. It just wasn't my type of party considering I was a self-proclaimed, party animal. Whenever I did attend a social gathering that didn't prohibit alcohol, I use to think I was being the life of the party when I was actually being a party pooper. My behavior inhibited everyone around me from enjoying themselves because I had drunk to the point where I become obnoxious. It became clear to me that I was not at all a "party animal", but rather a party pooper who caused problems. It was worse for the ones closest to me because when they needed me, I was either in a drunken coma or incoherent to what was going on. My ex-girlfriend once told me that she didn't feel safe with me because I could not protect her or our home when I was always in a drunken stupor or passed out. I had made a bad reputation for myself and it was very much deserving. I found myself pretending like I was happy and content with my life, but the truth was that I was hurting inside. I knew that I did not want to live the way that I was living anymore. It took for my life to reach an all-time low for me to begin to change. I was released from prison on parole for repeatedly driving under the influence of alcohol and within a month I was charged with another DUI. If convicted, it meant back to prison I'd go. So I did what I always did: I ran away from my problems. I didn't go to court for my DUI and I stopped reporting to my parole officer. I had two warrants issued for my arrest: one to return to prison and one to appear in court. I confined myself to my small apartment because going out was just too risky. After a couple of months, I got comfortable and every once in a while, I would go to the movies or out to eat with my girlfriend. Then I started going fishing all the time. I began to surround myself with anyone who wasn't prone to having confrontations with the law.

One day, I was drinking at home by myself and my cousin came over sloppy drunk. He asked me to go hang out with him and I declined his invitation. My cousin became really emotional as usual. He started giving me this lame sob story about how we had always been close. It had always been me and him against the world, and how lately I've been acting differently. I had been hanging out with everybody except him and I didn't make time for him anymore and blah, blah, blah. I usually had pity for him but on this particular day, I had none. I looked right into his pathetic face and told him, "We are not on the same page anymore. All you want to do is get drunk and I'm sick of it. The only reason why we have been close is because we both like to get drunk. Alcohol is our common denominator. We never do *anything* constructive or positive. We have been through a lot together, but none of it is good because it all has to do with us being drunken fools. The reason I don't go out with you is because you don't ever ask me to go anywhere worth going. All you want to do is go to somebody's house to get even more drunk and risk me getting another DUI."

When I finished talking to him, I could instantly feel the monkey on my back loosening its grip. I felt relief because for once in my life I said what I truly felt.

After my cousin left, I sat down and reflected on my life. As I thought about how much I let my life get out of order I became overwhelmed by a whole bunch of emotions that made me think about how unreliable and inept I had been. My heart began to cry out to my mother who I hadn't talked to in over a year. I had reached the lowest point in my life and shortly after that, I received some devastating news. Another warrant for my arrest had been issued for a crime I didn't commit. Now I was looking at spending the rest of my life in prison if found guilty. I wanted to turn myself in to get the matter resolved, but first I needed to obtain a lawyer. Every lawyer I contacted required at least twenty thousand dollars, *money I didn't have*, to try my case in court. I didn't know what to do or who to talk to about my personal matters. My mother heard about my situation and called me. During our conversation, she told me that she knew I was innocent. She said she would do anything she could to help and that she loved me. After hanging up the phone, I broke down and cried. My mother, who I accused my whole life of not being there when I needed her the most, was right by my side offering me her love and support. I didn't even have to explain my innocence to her because she already knew.

Eventually, the police picked me up on my warrants and I spent time in jail awaiting trial. When all was said and done, my innocence was proven. The time I spent in jail caused me to do a lot soul searching. I became aware of the broken heart that I had been carrying for all those years. I began to think back on how I lost my stepfather's side of the family. I realized that I really hadn't lost them, that in fact, I was the one that *cut them* out of my life. They always called me with happy birthday wishes and also sent me money on Christmas. I just *assumed* they didn't want anything to do with me. It was *me* who believed that they only sent me money for Christmas so I wouldn't feel badly when they sent it for my sister. It was *me* who stopped keeping in touch with them, causing us eventually to fall out of touch. I had begun to grasp how childish I was for holding a grudge against my mother all those years when my mother had raised me the best she could. How could I expect my mother to know what was going on with me when I never expressed my feelings to her? I always tried to be my mother's rock but I was weak. My mother had no idea how tore up I was inside. For all my mother knew, her son was all right. It was my sister who was going through some things and needed her undivided attention. How could I get mad at my mother for not sheltering me from my wrongs? How could I act as if my mother was the reason I was on my way to jail? She didn't break the law, I did. All my mother wanted was for me to do what was right. The more I soul searched the more I understood how wrong I was in my perception of the way things transpired. I began to see my wrongs for what they were, which was my wrong doings and not anyone else's. Once again, I began to sob as I thought about the grief I had caused my mother as well as myself. Suddenly, I knew what I had to do. I wrote my mother a letter and took full responsibility for my actions and asked for her forgiveness. I apologized for my wrong doings, pain, or grief I may have caused her. Not once did I blame her or tell her what she did wrong or could've done better because she raised me the best she knew how. My mind was made up to forgive my mother no matter what. When I sent the letter out, I began to have peace in my heart. All of the shame, hostility, and resentment started to leave me. The wounds of my past began to heal. My mother wrote me back and told me how much she loved me and that she accepted my apology. That was all I needed-right away the chains that kept me enslaved to my past were broken. I was finally free to move on with my life. At last, I felt the weight of King Kong lifted off my back.

How we *think and feel about ourselves* is the problem, not the drugs and alcohol. All that time, I thought my alcohol addiction was my problem but really my problem was with my life. In order for us to move on, we must let go of whatever is holding us back. Many people go wrong when they just try to deal with the addiction itself. You have to solve the problem in order to conquer the addiction. This is one of the reasons why treatment programs that are designed to help with alcohol and drug abuse don't always have lasting effects. Most individuals in the program can only abstain from drugs and alcohol for as long as they are without problems. Abstaining with problems causes many individuals to become stressed out. Listen to what the speaker at my first AA meeting had to say.

"Hi my name is Joe and I'm an alcoholic..." He then proceeded to tell his life story and finished up with, "...and I haven't had a drink in twenty-five years."

Huh?

Are you kidding me? Let me make sure I'm hearing this correctly: You haven't had a drink in twenty-five years and you still consider yourself alcoholic? I felt so sorry for Joe. For twenty-five years, Joe hadn't had a drop of alcohol, yet he was still bonded to alcohol. He felt that he had solved his alcohol addiction by substituting his drinking for AA meetings but it was obvious that Joe was still miserable. Nothing about Joe suggested that he was happy. He talked about his constant struggle to abstain from drinking and you could see visibly that he was stressed by it. Life would be so much easier for poor Joe if he would figure out what the *real* problem was.

We all have problems that are unique and different but there is a solution to all of our problems. It is imperative that you forgive those who have mistreated you, including your-self, and ask for forgiveness from those you have mistreated. When making an amends, you must take full responsibility for all of your wrongdoings which some may find hard to do. Some may find it hard to forgive someone they feel is still doing them harm. Instead of trying to do it all on your own, talk to someone whom you trust, is understanding, and that will offer you emotional support. If you don't feel safe or comfortable talking to someone, or you don't have any-one trustworthy to talk to, be willing to seek outside help. Seek out a social worker, psychiatrist, therapist, or maybe even a family or marriage counselor. You have to be willing to use all of the necessary resources to get your life in order.

When you are dealing with or have dealt with the prob-lem it makes it easier to conquer your addiction. Without the problem, you may find that you have no desire for drugs and alcohol, however, many people find treatment programs very helpful. They enjoy fellowshipping with fellow addicts. They enjoy the social interactions and all the feedback they receive from the group. They feel safe to express themselves without being judged or stereotyped. Don't get me wrong, there are treatment programs that have plenty of success. If you can incorporate treatment with the addition of solving your problems, I feel there can be even more success. With that being said, I don't agree with treatment programs that teach that alcoholism is an illness or disease that can't be cured. There are professional people who promote, "Once an alcoholic or drug addict, always one." I am not at all convinced of that.

I hate that they want you to admit, commit, and accept that way of thinking. If you have been told this, please listen to me, and listen very carefully: You are not an alcoholic or drug addict. You may be currently struggling or have strug-gled with alcohol and drugs in the past, however today is a new day. It is never too late to start a new chapter in your life. You may not be where you want to be in life, but you can still get there. I know you may have messed up, but you will make up for it. You are not a junkie or drunkie like they try to label you as. Not once did you say, "I'm going to grow up and be an alcohol and/or drug abuser." What you did say was, I'm going to be a good mother... a great husband... a doctor... a ball player... a singer, and I'm quite sure you can add many other things to the list. I promise you a junkie or drunkie isn't one of them. I'm sure you wanted to be great and that *is* what you are. It's never too late to right your wrongs, and the wrongs that can't be made right, you are never wrong for at least trying. People think they have you all figured out. They don't.

People may not trust you, they may be afraid of you or even resent you. They find you disappointing and embarrassing. They have very little respect for you, if any at all. But, can you blame them? I'm certain you feel it's very much deserving considering you have only showed them how bad you can be, rather than how good you really are. They don't know, but you and I both know there is awesome potential inside of you. They don't know about the war that is constantly going on inside you to do the right thing that you live through every day, but I do. I know how hard you want to do right and show your true colors. I know you want to get rid of those nasty stains, blotches and blemishes from your life. Now is the time. For those who have begun cleaning up their life, I'm not talking to you, but you are not an alcohol and/or drug addict. *You* are a survivor.

Now, if you are starting the cleansing process right now, don't try to be overly brave and do everything on your own. Reach out to someone for help. There is a good chance you may end up in a program that wants you to call yourself an alcohol and or drug addict. If that's the case, you go right along and say it so that you are complying with the program for sake of recovery. However, I don't want you to mean one bit of that bull crap. This is the truth. You were once an alcohol and or drug addict, but that was the old you. You are now a renewed individual. The new you is a good, respectable, and presentable person. You are many things but an alcohol and/or drug addict is no longer one of them. Don't you dare let them put that evil label on you. You march full esteem ahead with your recovery. Those professionals are too smart for their own good at times. They don't seem to recognize that the cure to alcohol and drug addiction is the individual himself. What they don't know, show them. As a matter of fact, we'll show them together.

I personally thought that when I conquered my alcohol addiction, my life would automatically get in order. Unfortunately, it was not instantaneous, I had a lot of work to do. I had spent over fifteen years developing bad habits and they didn't automatically disappear when my drinking stopped. I literally had fifteen years of my life to correct. I had many problems trying to understand my own actions. I wasn't doing what I wanted to do but I was doing everything that I hated doing. I had no control over myself, instead, I was a slave to my body because I did whatever it wanted me to do. In order for me to be the kind of man that I knew I was and that my family deserved, I had to gain back control over myself. Essentially, I discovered how to do things differently and I will like to share those things to you. I want to show you how to, *Impose Your Will Over Your Body*.

COMMUNICATION

Sticks and stones may break my bone but words will never hurt me. These are the words that can be heard across every grade school playground. This was one of the first lessons taught to me by my first grade elementary school teacher. The problem with that lesson was the fact that it was false. Words can really hurt some times. When used the wrong way, they can be dangerous and cause a lot of pain. Words have been known to destroy lives. The secret weapon behind most murders is nothing other than words. Yes, it's true, words are capable of murder. Words roll off the tongue like a sword engaged in battle. That very same tongue is a double edged sword that is capable of blessings and curses. Life and death is in the tongue. The tongue is a true indicator of the heart. The words that roll off our tongue reflect how we feel, what we stand for, what we think, where we come from, what we value, love, hate, desire, and in essence, what we are all about. We are guaranteed death, but our words can live forever. After reading this chapter you will have a greater understanding of the power of the tongue.

Blessings come from your tongue when you choose your words to be inspirational. Blessings come in the form of encouragement:

"You can do it."

"Don't give up!"

These blessings keep people motivated to keep going. It helps propel them toward their goal. Blessings come in the form of appreciation:

"Thank you for cooking dinner."

"I'm grateful that I can always depend on you."

These blessings show acknowledgement, recognition and that you are thankful. Blessings come in the form of exhilaration:

"Keep your head up."

"Good effort."

"You'll get them next time."

These blessings help up lift wounded individuals:

"You are a great speaker."

"You are good with your hands."

"You can be anything you want to be."

All of these words speak life, they help build others up. Words that come from the heart causing people to feel good or better about themselves are blessings. Many people go through their daily lives, hearing put down after put down. They feel torn and unappreciated for all the effort they put forth and all the good they do. They never receive recognition. They always feel like they are kicked while they're down. Sometimes, all it takes is a few kind words to pull these individuals out of the pits of hell. The tongue can just as easily be used to curse people as it is to bless them.

A curse inflicts destruction or punishment on a person and certain people don't hold back doing so. People are quick to lash out with the tongue causing evil and harm. They never take the time to consider what they are actually saying. Innocent children are cursed all the time, usually by a loved one. A single mother will often tell her son that he acts just like his father. The son has never met his father and all he knows of him is what his mother says about him. Which is: Your father is a bum, a liar, an irresponsible loser. He isn't a man, he's a little boy who's afraid of commitment. He would rather spend life in jail than take care of his son. With all that being said, what do you think the son thinks every time he does something wrong and his mother says, "You act just like your father?"

When the son becomes a man and find himself in jail, he automatically feels that jail is a part of his life because he has been told since day one that he acts just like his father. Of course, the mother didn't intend to curse her son, she was unaware of the powers of her tongue. A child you can always count on will do something wrong, we insist on calling them bad, not knowing that we are cursing them. Instead of us calling the child bad we should let them know that they are good kids who happen to do bad things. You can't correct a bad person or their ways. They are bad and bad people do bad things. The same goes for all the other titles we give people: liars-lie; thieves-steal; cheaters-cheat; killers-kill; and snakes bite. It's in their nature. A grown woman whose one and only time stealing was a quarter off her father's dresser when she was a child, does that make her a thief? By all means, no. She made a mistake and mistakes can be corrected. When you are convinced that you are good you will be good because it's in your nature. Now there may be a few wrinkles along the way, but nothing that can't be ironed out. Accept one of those wretched titles and you will fulfill the job description to that title.

You can also curse yourself. Say you can't do something and you never will because you believe you can't. It is as simple as that. Words are nothing to play with so choose your words carefully.

Words occasionally leave behind some nasty wounds. People will say some harmful things to you, to make themselves feel better or because they are having a bad day. Some people say stupid inappropriate things trying to be cute and funny. Then you have those ignorant people whose intentions are not to cause harm, but they say some of the stupidest things without understanding how insensitive they are being. Who left the mother fucking freezer open all night? Damn, all the food is thawed out. Whichever dumbass left the freezer open needs to start cooking because we aren't wasting shit. All the hairs on my body stood up while I was writing those sentences because this is how I actually talked at one point in time. This is how the people I hung around talked. It's sad to say, but this was considered the norm for me. I grew up thinking that it was okay to curse and use filthy language as long as I wasn't saying it in front of my elders. I had developed what you call a potty-mouth. Once I became an adult. I would use my potty-mouth in front of everyone except my children, my mother and sometimes I failed at that. Some people don't even hold to those standards. They talk however they want, whenever they want to whoever they want. One afternoon I awoke to my uncle's voice:

"I told yo ass you won't win again!"

"I told you, if I shutdown the pass you won't be able to do shit!"

"Got your ass now!"

"Who the fuckin' best?"

Now, when I went to sleep, the only people in my house were my seven-year-old son and my uncle. Now I'm behind my door puzzled, trying to figure out who is my uncle talking to. Then I heard my son say,

"Let's play again?"

"I bet you won't win again."

My uncle doesn't see anything wrong with the way he talks to his seven-year-old nephew. As you very well know, my uncle isn't alone. There are many others who see absolutely nothing wrong with the way my uncle talks to his nephew. This is the case of being very insensitive to what you say to others. The nasty words my uncle used were engraved in his mind from hearing them while growing up. Talking this way was second nature to him. What people fail to realize is that when someone uses foul language in every sentence, it indicates how ignorant they are. Their vocabulary is very limited which makes it hard for them to express themselves. You can get a clue as to where a person is from as soon as they open their mouth, by the way they sound and what they say. You can tell whether they are from the north, south, east, or west. You can tell if they are from a trailer park, a rich suburban neighborhood, the valley, or some inner city ghetto. Even if they are not from where they sound like they are from, I can guarantee you, someone they hang around is from there. By the words they use, you can get a sense of their intelligence level. One thing I know for certain is that loving, well respected people don't have pottymouths because they are polished individuals. They don't speak filth they speak very refreshing words.

I made the decision to stop using foul language and at first, I found it to be very difficult. The main problem I encountered was finding the right words to replace the foul ones with. It was as if I was speaking broken English because I would catch the bad word, but I would end up leaving it blank from lack of finding a better word to replace it with. Whenever I did find the right word, it sounded foreign rolling off my tongue. In the beginning, my goal was to stop cursing and I did, but I quickly realized that I had many more communication flaws that I needed to work on. I literally had to reprogram myself on how to communicate properly. Many of us find it hard to communicate effectively because we are full of bad feelings and have even worse thoughts. Therefore, every time we open our mouths we are expressing our horrible thoughts and feelings. View mind and emotions chapter for a more thorough thoughts and feelings explanation.

The main purpose for talking, is so we can express ourselves and understand others. We also talk for intimacy, to have fun and to entertain. You should never talk, just to be talking. There should always be meaning behind what you say. Here are a few pointers that helped me communicate more efficiently:

Spend More Time Listening- Almost everyone I found myself talking too, for some odd reason I always thought I knew what they were going to say. While they talked, I would eagerly wait for them to finish so I could talk. Sometimes I would rudely interrupt by answering their question or defending my point of view; only to find out I had no clue what they were going to say. I would end up answering a question they already answered or not answering a question at all. I would end up defending something that we agreed upon. Occasionally, midway during a person talking to me, I would realize that they weren't saying what I thought they were going to say, and had to ask them to repeat themselves or stand there and look dumb; pretending I heard what they said, praying they didn't need a response. A lot of times, I would be correct in my assumption and it still turned out to be awkward. As soon as I interrupted the speaker and began talking, the speaker would get aggravated and say, "Let me finish."

Trust me, it is hard to convince someone that they don't need to explain anymore because you already know what they are getting at before you have given them a chance to get at it. What I was doing was considered rude and disrespectful. I was being selfish. I wanted to express myself so badly, that I wasn't giving anyone else a chance to express themselves. For me to become a good speaker, I had to become an even better listener. I had to learn to hear others out before they would begin to try to hear me out. When I took the time to listen, I could hear what people were saying and not saying. I could tell how people felt even if what they said didn't match up. By listening to others, I began to understand that everyone doesn't want or need a response. Some people just need someone to listen to their opinions and views even if the conversation originally started with them asking me a question. I also learned how to not get myself caught up in foolish conversations. After listening to some people talk, I can tell right away that nothing they say, or are going to say is going to make sense. It's just a whole bunch of mumbo-jumbo and I don't have to waste any of my time trying to make sense out of what they are saying or try to convince them that what they are saying doesn't make sense. Some people just talk nonsense. They talk just to be talking, just to get some type of reaction out of somebody. Before I would get in frivolous quarrels with people because I didn't realize that they were just being foolish. By me taking the time to listen, my overall understanding of others is a lot clearer. You would be amazed at how much valuable information you can obtain by listening. For this very reason, you should listen more than you talk. The more you know about a person the more you can help a person. You should listen at least sixty percent of the time versus talking. That way when you do talk, the information that you obtained will cause your words to become more meaningful.

Talk To Everyone Like Your Brother- If I didn't care for you or need something from you, I didn't want to talk to you. You would have to gain my interest for me to engage in a conversation with you. I was notorious for one word answers and a demeanor that said, "Do not disturb. This is the usual type of conversation that strangers got from me:

Stranger: "Hello, how are you doing?"

Me: "Fine."

Stranger: "Beautiful day, isn't it?"

Me: "Yep."

Stranger: "I haven't seen you around before, did you just move here?"

Me: "Yes."

Stranger: "Do you have family here?"

Me: "Yep."

Stranger: "I use to walk out here all the time until I broke my leg a few months ago and today is the first day I've been able to walk without my brace."

Me: "Really."

Stranger: "Well, sorry to bother you, I got to try and fix this limp of mine. Nice to meet you. Have a good day."

Me: "You too."

That's it, that's all. That's all you would get out of me. My cold response gets the stranger to end the conversation quick. All I wanted the stranger to do was leave me alone. This poor, cold-hearted attitude caused me to miss out on a lot of amazing people. If I cared for the stranger or talked to them like they were a brother or sister, the conversation would have gone a lot different.

Stranger: "Hello, how are you doing?"

Me: "Fine, and you?"

Stranger: "I'm doing good. This is a beautiful day, isn't it?"

Me: "Yeah, I just moved into the blue house down the street. I moved here with my wife and two kids. We moved here from Illinois to enjoy the warmer climate. I usually try to walk an hour every day. Do you normally walk our here?"

Stranger: "I use to walk all the time until I broke my leg a few months ago and today is the first day I been able to walk without my brace."

Me: "Really? How did you break your leg?"

Stranger: "Well I coach pee-wee football and one of my boys made a good tackle on this kid and sent him flying out of bounds and his helmet landed right on my shin and cracked it. These old bones can't get out of the way like they used to."

Me: "Ouch! I bet that hurt. It's good you are back walking. How did you get into coaching football? I've always wanted to coach pee-wee football. I use to play in my younger days."

Stranger: "Well, you get into coaching by telling me you want to coach. I'm the president of the youth football league and we need a coach as we speak. What is your name?"

By me engaging in the conversation and talking to the stranger as I would a brother or sister, I ran into an opportunity and the conversation took only a minute of my time. The only thing I did differently was cared for the person I was talking to. I just showed a little empathy. Now when I talk to people, I try to put myself in their shoes and feel what they feel and see what they see. I try to always let people know a little about me. After all, I am the representor of me. My once cold attitude has turned into a warm and cordial attitude toward people. I'm always striving for a good relationship. I even treat little children as if they are important. I treat them the same as I would anybody else. We as individuals have a need to express ourselves. So give someone a minute of your time to do so. That's all it ever takes and you will meet some very amazing people that way. Remember this: You don't have to agree or disagree with anyone; everything isn't a debate. Our opinions may be different than others, but that doesn't mean we have to change them and neither does the other person unless they want to. You should make it a point of emphasis to always express yourself openly and honestly in an appropriate and responsible fashion. Now that doesn't mean spill your guts to any and every one, but make the proper decisions on who to talk to and how much to tell them personally about you. Trust yourself to determine who to trust. Show everyone brotherly love by giving them a chance to be heard.

Show Courtesy to Others- Treat everyone with respect. Make everyone feel of importance. Don't make people feel bad because they are fatter, thinner, taller, shorter, richer, poorer, etc. Sometimes you can talk to someone and make them feel as if you put hands on them. The whole conversation they feel like they must duck and dodge blows or take them to the head and gut. All while trying their best to avoid the low blows. Be open, honest and loving when talking. Every chance you get; you should pass out genuine compliments. I'm not talking about the insincere compliments that come with plenty of sarcasm and jealousy behind it because it isn't hard to tell that you are really saying. "You are not all that," or "I like you little red shoes." Those types of compliments don't make people feel better. People love sincere compliments because they are priceless gifts. Be careful with criticizing people. You should only give constructive criticism with good intentions. Most people have problems with people who are fault finders, so criticize tastefully.

My Yes Is My Yes and My No Is My No.[c]

There is absolutely no need for me to swear. I am what you call a man of his word. It's becoming more of a common occurrence for me to hear someone swear by something. From school play grounds to the work place all I ever hear is:

On my momma, I got all A's and B's last year.

On my kids, I can make lasagna from scratch.

I swear on a stack of Bibles, I haven't had a smoke.

On my life, I didn't drink your juice. On my mother-in-law's neighbor, dead dog, I'm not lying.

Really, what does all that mean? What does your mother, kids, or any of that other stuff has to do with you telling the truth? *Do not swear by your head for you cannot make one hair white or black.*[d] Besides that, you can't force God to take a life. You should rid yourself from swearing altogether. Every time you open your mouth, you should speak truthfully and be very concise. Far too often, we don't assert ourselves correctly. We don't say what we mean and we don't mean what we say. We try talking indirectly for fear of being rejected or hurting someone's feelings. You can't please everyone and it is okay to stand up for yourself without being aggressive. Don't beat around the bush about anything. If the answer is no, say no. Don't say, I don't know, maybe, we'll see or possibly when you know very well that the answer is no. It's your right to say no to whatever, whenever you like. If your answer is yes, mean it, own it, live up to it. Don't just commit to stuff loosely. When you give your word, hold yourself accountable. The worst thing you can do is be a disappointment when you don't have to. In most cases you can say no and change your mind later. When you are always truthful, it allows people to take your word for face value. After all, your word is everything. Keep it real, don't run around lying. Be trustworthy. If you can't speak the truth, don't speak at all. If there is one thing that I can't stand, it is people going around offering to tell you lies for no reason. I mean who do they think they are kidding, running around living in falsehood? Behind every lie, there is the bold face truth. You may get away with many lies, but once one lie is discovered, your words mean nothing. One lie can tarnish everything you say or have ever said. You should always keep it one-hundred, meaning, being real and genuine, not a factitious phony.

Avoid Gossiping At All Cost- The only exception is spreading good news. Don't go around putting someone's dirty laundry in the streets. If you must put any laundry in the streets, make sure it's clean. You gain absolutely nothing by being the bearer of bad news. I know people who can't wait to tell you what somebody else has done wrong or what's going wrong in somebody else life. They do this to try and draw all the attention off themselves. They don't want you to even catch a glimpse of the messed-up things going on in their lives. Therefore, they can't wait to spread what they call, juicy information. Most of the time, it is a fabricated half-truth, or their opinion that they pass off as a fact. The gossiper is a very dangerous individual. They cause the most problems and have you caught up in the most mess. They will coerce you to dislike people you don't even know. A gossiper will tell you that your neighbor Jim is cheating on his wife because he sneaks out to see his mistress every night at three o'clock in the morning. You go for months not liking Jim. Every time you see his car easing out of the driveway at three o'clock in the morning, you're overwhelmed with anger. You avoid speaking to him. You invite every neighbor on the block except for Jim to your cook outs. Until one night, you have trouble sleeping and decide to go to the nearest gas station for some junk food. As you are putting your late-night snacks on the counter, you notice that Jim is the cashier. Jim immediately says hello and comments that you that you must be having an unusual late night snack attack because he has been working the grave yard shift, part time for nine months now, and he has never seen you at this time of hour. All this time, you thought he was cheating on his wife because of what the gossiper said. Oops, your bad. Gossipers cause conflict amongst groups. They're always the ones behind the he-said-she-said, crap. They are the ones who cause everyone to look at you strangely when you walk into a room. Give people a chance to find out who people are on their own. The characteristics you may dislike about someone, may be loved by another. If you can't say something nice, don't say anything at all. Keep detrimental information to yourself. Avoid causing unnecessary problems. Everything isn't meant to be spread around. When someone confides information in you, that doesn't mean run and tell someone else. If they wanted them to know they, would have told them. It's hard to have a healthy relationship with someone who can't hold water. Spread good news and good news only. Always speak up for yourself. People tend to only want to repeat bad things about you. Every chance you get, you should let people know everything good about you. The best things about you should be told by the person who knows you best and that person is you. Telling people the bad things about you is not at all considered being humble. All you are doing is giving people ammunition to use against you. Stop with calling yourself stupid and dumb. Stop saying bad things about yourself because the more you hear the bad things, they will become ingrained in your mind and become how you think about yourself. Sometimes, I really don't think that people understand what they say. There has been a bad epidemic of women calling themselves a bitch. A bitch is a malicious and spiteful woman, meaning you only have intentions to cause harm. Is that what you really mean? Because that is what you really said. I'm inclined to believe you because after all, you know yourself best. If you treat yourself bad and talk badly about yourself, how do you expect everyone else to treat you? My guess is like a stupid, dumb bitch. Do you get my point? If you want people to respect you and take you seriously start by respecting your-self. There are too many people who love to say bad things about you, don't add yourself to the list. Speak good things about yourself and others and you will be a blessing in dis-guise.

EMOTIONS

ॐ∞ல

There is a surreal effect when traveling up an elevated track of a rollercoaster ride. There's a whole bunch of mixed emotions that run through you at this time. You feel courageous for even getting on. As the coaster climbs up the incline, you start to feel scared and full of regret. You wonder how did you trick yourself to get on the ride. You know that at the top of the slope, the coaster will start to descend at a very fast pace. You are suddenly not sure if your heart can handle the ride. You want to get off. You wish the coaster will stop but you have no control over it. The only person who has control is the seventeen-year-old operator, who loves to see the look of terror on all the passengers faces. You gather your pride together and put a smile on your face. The coaster arrives at the top of the slope, and you start to dread being on the coaster. All the pride you gathered together is lumped up in your throat. You try to endure the fright as the coaster heads down the track. The coaster plunges steeply down the slope and the fright becomes unbearable. Your heart feels like it's going to jump out of your chest, you swallow your pride and scream. The coaster without notice, slows down and changes direction. You are relieved that your heart is still in place. You realize that you endured the most frightful part of the ride. You throw your arms up and let out a yell of excitement. Within a snap the coaster zooms down a couple of drops-and-turns and is heading sideways to a dark cave. You have an uneasy feeling come over you as you approach the cave. It looks too small to let anyone over five feet enter without knocking their head off. You duck your head down in your shoulders, close your eyes, and brace for impact, nothing happens. You open your eyes and to your surprise, you made it through the cave, alive with your head intact. You feel a sense of relief immediately. Suddenly, the roller coaster propels forward and your body is thrown back against your seat. You are scared to death as you are looking at the sky as the coaster charges over 100 feet up a loop on the track. You begin to have an anxiety attack as you are turned upside down heading around the loop of the track. The coaster comes out of the loop, slows down abruptly, and comes to a hasty stop. You exhale as you erase the worried look off your face and change it to a look of satisfaction. You feel alleviated as the ride begins to propel forward to its end. Other passengers applaud for an encore. You on the other hand have a whole bunch of mixed emotions going through your head. You are uncertain how you feel at the present time, because you just went through a whole bunch of ups-and-downs, twist-and-turns, and you are finally starting to level off. This is what most people consistently go through emotionally.

Majority of us are on an everlasting emotional roller coaster ride. We constantly go through the highs-and-lows, risk-and-rewards, and never attain stability because we allow our emotions to run wild. We allow our emotions to drag us along for a ride against our will.

The human emotions are very complex. They sometimes cause us to behave in ways that we normally wouldn't if our emotions were not involved. They cause us to overreact and overlook certain situations. Our emotions let us know how we feel about ourselves and others. They determine how we treat things. They cause us to feel inferior and superior to others.

Emotions can alter our looks. Sad people tend to have sadness written all over their face. Their body physically slumps, their forehead becomes wrinkled, the corners of their mouths droop, their eyes cast down, and they look as if it would hurt to smile. Truly happy people tend to smile a lot. They stand tall, happy, and proud.

Some of us have emotional ties to difficult past situations that hinder us from progressing forward. If we were to gain control of our emotions; we would be able to use our difficult past to work to our advantage. Too often we let others choose how we feel. We put up with our angry, grouchy, boss for eight hours. Then we come home to our families angry and grouchy. We always put on different facades to please others, all because we don't have our emotions in check. As passengers on an emotional roller coaster ride, we constantly blame our actions on the way we feel. I cheated on my spouse because I didn't receive enough affection. I broke the phone because I was mad. I got drunk because I was feeling down and out. These aren't factual excuses. These are just the ways the passengers of the emotional roller coaster try to rationalize it. As strange as it may seem, you don't do what you do because you feel the way you feel. You feel the way you feel because of what you do. I feel guilty because of the affair I'd been having. I'm mad because I broke the phone. I feel down and out because I got drunk. When you decide to love someone, the feeling will follow whether it was there before or not. This is what happens when you decide to be the operator of the emotional roller coaster, versus the passenger. We should not allow our emotions to get the best of us. It's good to let our emotions be understood but we should never allow our emotions to run our lives. If you permit your emotions to lead you in events and circumstances, you are vulnerable to being victimized. Having a victim mentality will prevent you from taking advantage of great opportunities.

You consciously and unconsciously make decisions based on past experiences. I won't love another man because my ex was abusive towards me. I won't learn how to work a computer because everyone will call me illiterate. I won't go work-out with a personal trainer at the gym because I know I will get laughed at. We must understand that having a victim mentality is a choice. You can hold yourself back or you can have a look-at-me-now story. I was overweight, out of shape, and feeling depressed but look at me now. I got my body in great shape and I look and feel good. Our will is constantly dealing with many of our emotions. For us to have control of ourselves, we must learn to control our emotions.

Love is the most powerful emotion that we possess. Love is so powerful, it it hard to explain what love truly is. Many people consider falling in love, actual love. When actually, love is a choice. I have never met anyone who chose to fall on purpose, however, people always fall unintentionally. When you fall in love you may get love all over you but it doesn't mean you have love in your heart. This is why many people get involved with people they don't actually love. They just thought they did at the time because they were covered "in-love" from the fall. When you first got with your significant other, you were in-love with them. You were in love with their voice, there cocky attitude and constant attention. You even found yourself in love with the smell of their breath in the morning and not knowing exactly why, you loved cleaning up after them. After sometime, the love you were covered in starts to wear off and you find yourself no longer in love. Suddenly, you hate their cocky attitude and constant attention. You wish they were humbler and would give you more space. You wish they would brush their teeth in the morning before trying to pillow talk. You especially wish they would start cleaning up after themselves. You begin to ask yourself if you are with the right person because you find your significant other, not so significant anymore. More like bothersome and irritating. Everything they do now annoys you. You no longer want to be around or spend time with them. You try your best to avoid them. You work overtime, stay tuned into the TV, and spend more time at the bar. You find yourself falling in love with someone else. Now you're having an affair with someone you think you love and in a relationship with someone you thought you loved. All of this can be avoided if we take the time to understand love. Love was explained best by an author named Paul, who was writing to a group of confused people. Paul wrote, *"Love is patient, love is kind. It does not envy, it does not boast, it is not proud. It is not rude, it is not self-seeking, it is not easily angered, it keeps no record of wrongs. Love does not delight in evil but rejoices in the truth. It always protects, always trusts, always hopes, always perseveres."e*

When Paul wrote this, he was speaking of true love. Not the romantic kind of love that is insufficient because it is anchored by emotions. Not the, I-love-what-you-do-for-me kind of love, because love is lost when you can no longer do. Paul was talking about the kind of love that promotes happiness in others and finding joy in their happiness. Don't get me wrong, falling in love and being in love are not bad things. In fact, it is a beautiful feeling. However, it is a temporary feeling that holds no worth unless you decide to actually love the person. Love is not something that just happens, it's something you have to work hard at. It requires your time and energy. You have to learn how to love. If love is to be moral, it is a matter of all or nothing at all. Therefore, you have to learn to love people for the way they actually are, not who they can potentially be. To love someone, you must accept them for the way they are right now. Do not expect too much or too little from them. You can love flawed people without loving their flaws. Deep down with in our will, we have a passionate commitment to love all that is good, true and beautiful. We can dislike their flaws, hate all their bad ways and delight in all their good, all while loving them. Nobody is perfect, but there is the perfect person for everyone if they would only realize that nobody's perfect.

In one of my earlier relationships, when my girlfriend and I were only friends, walking through a park, talking and enjoying each other's company. Out of the blue, she tells me she loves me and left a lot of space for me to tell her I love her back. Unfortunately, I didn't feel that way at the time, so I didn't respond to her statement that was secretly her way of asking me a question. When my girlfriend noticed that I didn't respond and that I wasn't going to. She said, "stop acting like you can't tell me you love me; you can tell me. I wanted to not respond again but by the sound of her voice and look on her face, I knew she needed me too. I took a deep breath then explained the best I could my true feelings.

"I can't say that I love you because I don't feel that way right now. I mean, I like you a lot but…"

With a big smile on her face, my girlfriend immediately cut me off and said, "Boy, you love me." She said those four words as if implying that I had just told her the biggest tale she has ever heard. The reason why I couldn't tell her I love her was because I didn't think we knew each other long enough. It was too soon for me to love her. We hadn't even made love how could I be in love with someone I'd never made love with? There was still a lot I didn't know about her. On the other hand, my girlfriend had already made a conscious decision to love me. She loved me for the way I was right then, flaws and all. She did not love me for what I could potentially be, but you better believe every time I reached or exceeded my full potential, it gave her a reason to love me more. She also knew that I loved her. The truth is, I did love her. I had made my decision unconsciously. I had every intention on working hard at loving her. However, I did not think that it was possible for me to love her so soon. At that point in my life, I thought you could only love someone after a certain amount of time has passed and under certain conditions, which is not the case at all. I know now that you can love someone at first sight. I was always one to disagree with that theory until I realized that love was a choice. If you want to see an example of love at first sight, buy a child a puppy. Trust me, that child will immediately love that puppy unconditionally.

Sometimes, we love people we have never met. Many of us have family members we have only heard of, yet we love them because they are a part of us. We make unconscious decisions that allow us to love naturally. Our will wants us to love everyone. Meaning your neighbor, mail carrier, supervisor, the police officer who wrote you a speeding ticket, all your enemies, and everyone else. However, we make it hard to love others because we have problems loving our self. We are consistently neglecting, harming, and not taking good care of ourselves. To love others, we have to accept our self and the separateness of others. We also need to receive love and to be cared for. Which is why it's impossible to love anyone if you don't love yourself.

It's hard to show love to those around you when deep inside, you hate yourself. Many of us need to do ourselves a favor and pick ourselves up. If your self-esteem is low, you need to develop a better opinion of yourself.

Society is always misleading us to believe that for us to be somebody, we have to look, dress, and talk a certain way. When we try to live up to societies expectations, we are always going to fail. You can never be like someone else but you can be a better you.

People are doing the craziest things in their pursuit to be, and look like someone else. Plastic surgeons are making unnecessary money on breast implants, butt implants, Botox, and many other forms of surgery. You must accept who you are as a person. Be proud of all your physical features especially your distinct ones. Blaming others for your low self-esteem is a waste of time. You have low self-esteem because you treat yourself that way. You have to treat yourself like somebody if you want others to also. You can't wear your clothes all sloppy, keep a messy house and say, "That's just the way I am." That's just the way you choose to be. There is a better you. Start dressing like you would like to dress. Don't tell yourself that you can't start until you lose X number of pounds, or any other excuse. Start right now. I promise you that you will feel so much better. Clothes don't make a person but cleanliness, neatness, and pressed shirts count. You must dress for success. All the things you love to do, do it. *I can't*, is not a good excuse either because the truth is, you can if you want to. Don't waste your time drowning in self-pity. Concentrate on all your triumphs and not your failures. Dismiss all your negative expectations and destructive thoughts and beliefs. Don't let people make you feel like you are a bad or worthless person because there is an amazing person inside of you. Stop telling yourself what you are not and start owning up to everything that you are. All your past mistakes are in the past. Today is a new day. It is time to move on. If you start believing you are somebody, you will start to see it and everyone else will too. Integrity plays a major role in our opinion of ourselves. Don't do anything in the dark that you would be ashamed of coming to light. I must catch myself from doing shameful things all the time. There have been small things like not washing my hands after using the restroom. As soon as I leave the restroom, I start to feel shameful. My mind starts to wonder did anyone see me, and I end up going back to wash my hands. If someone of importance was to observe me not wash my hands it would be damaging to my self-esteem. Not because I'm ashamed of myself, but I'm ashamed of the way I appeared to the person who observed me. What we do when no one is around does matter. Therefore, it is in our best interest to do what is morally right even if no one is watching. Always follow your dreams and not the dream of someone else. Just because everyone in your family graduated from the University of Illinois doesn't mean you have to. Be what you want to be. You are the captain of your own ship.

Spend more time helping others. When you consistently volunteer the good in you to others, all of your needs and problems hold less weight on you. Show courtesy and be compassionate to others. Treat all people the same. Give them the same love you give to yourself. When you have a better opinion of yourself it allows your lovely personality to shine through. You no longer try to dominate or shy away from conversations. You no longer try to prove how smart and fun you are. You are not always negative and dry. You are not arrogant and stuck up. You don't try to make people feel inferior to you. Many of your bad personality traits will slowly change the higher your self-esteem rises. The more confidence you have in yourself the better you would get along with others. You will no longer say, I can't get along with so-and-so because we have conflicting personalities.

Instead, you will have a willing personality and not allow your emotions to affect their distinctive character. You will become a wonderful person to be around, when you give up putting on all the different costumes in your effort to be like someone else. Just be yourself. The things we concern ourselves with daily doesn't even matter.

There is no point in worrying about things that don't matter. Worrying only leads to anxiety. Anxiety will have you feeling uneasy, apprehensive, and extremely tense. Now it's okay to feel nervous. Nervousness just shows that you have respect for the opinion of others. Although, there is nothing good about anticipating misfortune and danger all the time. When you feel anxiety come over you, relax and direct the attention off yourself to others, by not worrying about your problems. Follow the songs advice that says, "Don't worry, be happy."

If you've learned anything from me, you should know that people are as happy as they choose to be. I know you probably feel that you are an exception because of what you went through growing up, how you had to do everything on your own, how somebody you loved so much did you so wrong, and how every other unfortunate thing that has happened to you. You have every right to sulk about your unfortunate situations, if you want to feel sad and depressed. Despite that, if you want to be happy, think about all the good in your life and be happy. Be happy about all the good you will bring to others lives. Some people look for happiness in all the wrong places. Some are victims of being bullied so they became police officers and other positions of power to bully the bully. Some look for happiness in material goods. Some feel lonely and unloved and turn to gangs. You may find temporary happiness in these places, but, the truth is you will remain unfulfilled. All the unnecessary emotional behavior patterns you learned growing up, unlearn. When someone passes away, you don't have to be sad, you can choose to be happy for all the good times you shared with the person. You should always try to turn all bad news into good news or at least better news. Don't be set in your ways, choose to be happy. You might have to leave a lot of people you deal with behind because some people love misery.

Many of us are miserable because we penalize ourselves for guilty feelings. We constantly blame ourselves for every little thing, which generates shame, discouragement, and resentment toward ourselves. I'll be the first to admit, I have done many things in my life time that I'm not proud of. I've done many things that I'm ashamed of. It's only natural for me to feel this way because I have more dirt on myself than I do anybody else. In-order for me to be able to live with myself, I had to forgive myself. I had to forgive myself often for everything my conscience convicts me of. Forgiveness sets us free from the past. By not condemning myself and having compassion for myself, it allowed me to always pick myself up and move on. Forgiving others is what I found to be the biggest challenge.

My children's mother had a bad habit of making my children unavailable to me when I'd made plans for us. I always let her know my plans ahead of time. One time, I told her K-MART had a good deal on family portraits so I scheduled an appointment for me and the kids to take pictures on Saturday the 17th, which was a few weeks away. I told her I'd pick them up at 8:30am Saturday morning and she said okay. I called the night before to confirm our arrangement and make sure everything was all right. Which she assured me it was. I showed up on time to pick up my babies from their mothers, only to find out they were not there. Not only were they not there, they were in separate cities.

"How did all this transpire between last night and this morning?" Is what I asked their mother. She gave me some lame excuse like, "They got a big family. I can't control who plans to be with them."

I left feeling frustrated and disappointed about her ruining my plans. I use to wonder how on earth could she be so cruel toward me. Besides, I always let her drop the kids off with me at the last minute, so she can make it to her late-night dentist appointment that no one else in the world can get. To make matters worse, this wasn't the only time something like this happened. She always found ways for me to waste my hard-earned money and screw up my quality time with my kids. Over time, I developed a grudge and did not want to forgive her for the way she treated me. I stopped answering all calls that came from her home. When she tried to drop the kids off expectantly, I turned her down. I told her I had something to do, even if I didn't. In the long run, all I ended up doing was hurting myself and my children. Some of those calls I ignored were my babies trying to talk to their daddy. The times when I said they couldn't come over because I was busy, really hurt me because I wanted to be around them. My attempt to teach her a lesson and make her apologize for how she wronged me, backfired. All I did was become controlled by her. She was still winning the battle because she wasn't worried about me at all. I on the other hand, was worried about how my babies were doing. I had learned important lessons from all this; vengeance is unnecessary, two wrongs don't make a right and I should forgive her for her cruel ways. I should not have let her dictate my relationship with my kids based off my emotions. I should have made the best out of every situation and took care of the problem legally. Some people are hard to deal with, you must forgive them ahead of time because they never have good intentions. You ought to forgive them whether they deserve it or not. No point in being depressed because of someone else. They are not walking around depressed because of you. I can't count how many times I have witnessed someone get all stressed out over someone they hardly knew doing them wrong. I went to a fast food restaurant with a friend of mine. She ordered some type of value meal and she specifically said no tomatoes on her burger. When we arrived home, she unwrapped her burger and saw big, red, slimy, tomatoes hanging off. Immediately she transformed into the exorcist and started ranting:

"Why would they put tomatoes on my burger and I told them not too. I hate tomatoes! What if I was allergic to them? Are they trying to kill me? We got to go back there. I'm not eating this."

I mean she went on and on about some tomatoes. She was so upset that she was aging by the minute. I witnessed her silky black hair turn into a head full of gray right before my eyes. I convinced her that it was just a waste of gas to drive back there for a burger with no tomatoes, when she could pick them off herself. She was so upset by this, that she threw the burger away and refused to eat anything at all. She decided to stay upset and hungry. She could have realized that everyone makes mistakes, and even if it wasn't a mistake, she could have forgiven them, took the tomatoes off herself and enjoyed her meal. Instead, she chose to be stressed on an empty stomach, causing me to gain a few pounds because there was no way I was going to let her throw her fries away.

Don't let people get the best of you. Be quick to forgive because hostility causes stress. Forgive all the things that are behind you and reach for the things ahead of you. I don't mean to erase all recall, but don't hold anything against someone when you forgive them. Get rid of all grudges daily and forgive everyone before you close your eyes at night.

Don't just excuse, tolerate or put up with. Forgive and wish them the best so you can move on with your prosperous and fruitful life.

Learn to be under control always. People don't make you angry, you make yourself angry. You say to yourself, if she raises her voice at me one more time I'm gon' go off. The truth is, you make yourself angry when somebody raises their voice at you. Anger is always a bad thing unless it is righteous anger, which is a passionate displeasure in evil.

Suspicious anger is the most inappropriate form of anger. A lot of times, we let anger get a hold of us because we instantly react to the situation instead of respond. Your boss might tell you, we no longer need you at this position causing you to cut him off, get angry and say somethings you regret. You must learn to respond appropriately. When you respond, you create an outlet to deal with the situation. Who knows, your boss was probably going to tell you, "We no longer need you at this position because I promoted you to a higher position." However, you allowed yourself to get angry and told your boss where he could shove this job before he could finish his statement. When it was all said and done, you were angry for no reason. Suspicious anger is the worst form of anger. Whomever possess this kind of anger can drive themselves insane because of things that may or may not have happened.

I knew a guy who was angry at his wife because he thought she was cheating on him. His wife had decided to make changes in her life for the better. She gave up smoking and drinking. She joined a gym and spent four hours a week with a personal trainer. She maintained a healthy diet and made a hobby out of bowling and walks around town. She traded in her wardrobe full of granny panties, sweat suits and dusters, for a wardrobe full of sexy garments like lingerie, and heels. Not only did she dress sexy on special occasions, she dressed sexy every day. She brightened up her beautiful face with just enough make up to bring out her looks. She smiled more and looked happier. She now had a firm butt and toned thighs. He loved how gorgeous she looked in her new outfits. He couldn't figure out why the new behavior, no matter how hard he tried to keep an open mind, support, and trust her. However, he couldn't stop asking himself, who is she trying to look sexy for? Who is she sleeping with? Why does she go to the gym instead of watching her favorite TV show? Over time, things started to get messy. He thought she was having an affair. He began spying on her and could never catch her behaving inappropriately. This only made matters worse, when he could not catch her in the act because he found himself mad all the time. He finally convinced himself that she was cheating when he found extra cash in her purse after snooping through it. He was certain that her new found love was giving her money. It never occurred to him that she had extra cash because she no longer spent money on cigarettes, booze, and junk foods. He had it in his head that she was going to leave him for a guy with more money. He started working overtime at his job to bring home more bacon. On the other hand, he became very controlling. He didn't want her to go to the gym or bowling. He wanted her to stay at home. She complied but it made her unhappy. She found herself wanting a long island iced tea and a smoke. She didn't want to go back down the road to his suspicions. He just couldn't figure out that she was tired of destroying her body. He lost his wife, not because of something she did, but, because of something he thought she did or was doing. He allowed his emotions to get the best of him.

Suspicious anger is often confused with jealously. Jealousy is what we feel when we are afraid of losing someone's meaningful connection. It is how we feel when we believe someone has something of a greater value than us. It is based off something unlike suspicious anger which is based off a suspicion. Jealousy under control can be a good thing. If you can openly talk about, why and what makes you jealous, you can let someone know how much they matter to you. Jealousy can also let you know how much someone or something means to you. It can give us something to laugh about. Nevertheless, if jealousy is left unchecked, it can make you act uncharacteristically. It opens the door for many other emotions to take a strangle hold of you. Jealousy, not under control can become dangerous and even deadly. To better control jealousy you must be secure with yourself. You have to understand; people will have somethings of greater value than you. You need to not worry about what they have and be content with what you have.

Sitting around dwelling on somebody else good fortunes evolves into bitterness and envy. Allowing yourself to let these things marinate your mind will turn you into a hater. If you don't know what a hater is, let me be the first to explain. A hater doesn't want to see you do well and if you are, they are eagerly waiting for you to fall and love when it happens. A hater will magnify the smallest blemish into a major flaw. They never want you to do better than them, they always want you at least a step behind. Haters are everywhere and their goal is to do nothing other than seek and destroy. Haters are in your workplace. They try to make you feel bad by calling you a brownnoser.

They say, "You think you own the place. You only get paid x number of dollars. You act like you live here. They don't pay you more for doing more. You are going to be worker of the decade. You only got the position because you're always sucking up."

They say these things in their attempt to discredit all your hard work. Haters are at our schools calling us geeks and nerds for getting good grades, calling us dumb and stupid for asking questions of relevance. Haters are at our churches talking about how people swear, smoke, drink, fornicate, listen to the devils' music, go to the bars, and clubs all week then show up to church to worship. Those hypocrites! Do they think they are without sin? Isn't church for the sinners? Some of those very same people can be found committing those same sins in the church. Do they not know that they are pushing some of the most beautiful people away? I'm sure the pews in church will be empty if it was for the righteous only. Haters are the ones who try to get you hooked on drugs and alcohol. They look at you and can't stand to see you clear headed and sober. They want you to be defiled because you are too pure for their liking. They want you to be tarnished, no matter how many times you say no, it won't stop them from trying to convince you to take something you don't need. They do all this because they feel uncomfortable with you unless you are on their level or beneath them. If you become addicted to drugs or alcohol, they are the ones that call you a junkie or alcoholic that they no longer want to be around. Haters are the ones that tell you it's too late to go back to school or start a new career. They crush you dreams of being somebody or doing something great. Haters want you to get rid of your car that you own that has been reliable getting you and your family from A to B; get a new car and make payments that you can't afford. They want you to get a bigger home, wear designer clothes and be stuck in debt like them. Haters are the ones constantly nagging in your ear about how you and your lover shouldn't be together. Every chance they get they are planting seeds: "You don't have to put up with that. Your lover doesn't care about you. Your lover only cares about themselves. Your lover doesn't make enough money. I wouldn't let that person text my lover. Allowing your lover to be with so-and-so is just opening doors for them to cheat. You make more than your lover; you need someone to at least make what you make. I wouldn't let my girl wear that outside the house. A man isn't supposed to cook and clean the woman is.

They try their best to transport all their insecurities to your head. They want you to be mentally unstable. They will do any and everything to separate you and your better half, and they have the nerves to wonder why they are single and miserable. Haters are the ones who don't want to see you healthy and fit. They always have something negative to say. When you are overweight trying to lose weight, they say: "Trying to eat healthy is just a waste of time, you are not going to lose all that weight. You can walk to Mexico on that treadmill and you will still be fat. Some people were meant to be big. Why are you trying to be skinny?"

They say this to try and stop you in your tracks. Most of these haters are out of shape and they can't afford for you to get in shape because it makes them look even more out of shape. They try to convince you that being in shape, or what they call skinny, is a bad thing. They will try to convince you that they love being overweight, or well proportioned, big boned, voluptuous or curvaceous, whatever what they call it. Tell them to save it! If that was true, they would not complain about how much their back and knees hurt, all the time. They wouldn't cry to you about how hard it is to find clothes that fit. They wouldn't complain about how exhausted and beat they are; and how they wish that they could play with the kids. Don't let them stop you from getting that body in good condition.

When you are in great physical condition, what they call skinny, they say: "You need to put some meat on them bones. You can do all the pushups in the world and you will never be as big as the Hulk. Why do you need to work out? Who are you trying to look good for?"

That's the one I personally hear all the time, "Who are you trying to look good for?"

"Uh... myself."

I want to look good and feel good for myself. I exercise to maintain optimum health. Duh... It also humors me when haters try to make you feel underweight because they are overweight. They say, "Don't nobody want skin and bones." Some people may not, but don't nobody want an out of shape, diabetic, who gets out of breath when walking up a flight of stairs, who accrues huge medical expenses due to their overweight problems, and cost a fortune to feed either. The truth is, they wish they were in your shoes, they wish they could feel and look like you. First thing they want to say to you is, "You think you are all that." No, you think I'm all that. I know I'm not all that. Which is why I exercise and eat healthy to try and obtain some of that. Whatever "that" is.

Ladies, please do not let haters dissuade you from showing off your body. If you have the body to flaunt, by all means, flaunt it. If you want to dress sexy by all means, do it. I'm not talking about the Janet Jackson at the Super Bowl type of provocative: If it's offensive to others, don't wear it, and yes, a 5ft' 4", 400lb women in a string bikini would be very offensive. However, if you look good in what you wear, wear it.

As for you older women, please do not let these younger girls tell you that you are too old to wear something that you look just as good or better than them in. I would rather see Halle Berry in a sexy dress than most 20 year olds.

Keep all of the joy thieves out of your life. Anybody who doesn't want you to do good, look good, and feel good are haters. The better you do throughout your life, the more critics you will acquire. Let the haters hate, as a matter of fact, give them more to hate about. If you don't have any critics there is something wrong with you.

The last emotion I want to get into is pride. Pride disables people from their full potential. They began to feel they are better than what they are, they over estimate themselves, they become a legend in their own mind. Not only do they know it all, they can do it all. They think they have it all figured out to the point where they feel they must straighten everybody else out. It's just a matter of time before they're thrown off their high horse, lying flat on their back in failure. Never attempt to get on that high horse. No one in the world can ride it. Everyone who has tried was thrown off. Keep a humble mind. Know that you are not better than anybody else without feeling lower than anybody else. You don't have to brag, boast, or toot your own horn. When deserving, somebody will toot it for you.

Every moment of our lives, we have to deal with the emotions discussed in this chapter and many more. All our emotions can be controlled. Our job is to control or rid ourselves from all the negative emotions. Hard work and no rest aren't the only things to have you tired. Negative emotions drain you to the point of exhaustion. When you allow yourself to be worried, frightened, or nervous, you become worn out. It is very tiring to be angry and think negative thoughts. Carrying out your will is impossible when you are fatigued and feeling woozy from the emotional roller coaster. If you don't already, be sure to govern all of your emotions because they have a major influence on your will.

ENTERTAINMENT

❧

Clearly, man's best friend is no longer a dog but an entertainment system. When folks aren't eating, sleeping or taking a crap, chances are they're watching TV, listening to music, playing a video game or interacting with social media.

Children now days are being raised by the social media, television and radio. Young men and women are learning how to be adults based off what they see from these forms of entertainment. The days of seeing kids outside playing tag, jumping rope and climbing trees are over. I here parents say all the time, "I don't know where Junior learned how to talk like that, because no one in our family talks that way." Well if it's not the parent, it's probably the TV that he's in front of all day. I find it kind of comical when parents arc having an adult conversation while Junior is present in the room; and one parent tells Junior to go and watch TV in his room because grown folks are talking; and Junior goes in his room and hears conversations on TV that are more unfitting for him than his parent's conversation in the other room. Cartoons are no longer innocent so don't be naïve into thinking that because it's a cartoon, it is suitable for children. Cartoons just aren't the same anymore. You use to be able to turn to any cartoon and about the worst you would see was a cat dropping a piano on his foot while trying to catch a mouse, or a skunk trying to woo another skunk, which were all appropriately funny. Now, if you turn to a random cartoon, there's a chance that your ears will be flooded with profanity and you see a scene that you would only expect Ron Jeremy or Heather Hunter to be acting out. Television is where kids grow up too fast. They're introduced to things they are not yet ready for. It's where lust begins to creep into their hearts. They will try to emulate whatever they see on TV. There isn't a kid in the world who watched the original Karate Kid and did not wish they were Daniel-San. As soon as the movie ended, every kid in the universe immediately did the famous crane pose. I know I did. I used to watch Teenage Mutant Ninja Turtles as a kid and fantasize about being a secret crime fighter who lives in the sewers eating pizza all the time. I watched a documentary on Dr. Martin Luther King Jr and I wanted to be a preacher and civil rights activist when I grew up. I also watched Scarface and desired to be just like Tony Montana. I wanted to be a feared drug lord who didn't take any body's crap. I began to crave money, cars, clothes and women. This is a prime example why kids shouldn't watch rated R movies. Speaking of rated films and TV shows, you may disagree with the age they deem appropriate for certain films and shows. My daughter at six years old fell in love with the show, That's So Raven and Hannah Montana. These shows covered topics such as dating, sex and drugs with a good educational message intended. Some ratings suggested that the shows were for ages seven and up. Although my daughter was only six, I still didn't feel that the shows would have been appropriate if she were seven. Do you think age seven is the appropriate time to teach your child about those topics? Its TV shows like these where our children pick up ways to lie themselves out of situations. I'm not going to say that you are wrong if you feel that these types of shows are appropriate for a seven-year-old.

However, I feel you should be the first to talk to your child about topics like sex, drugs and dating. That way your child is not misled by all the false information that goes around. It's your job to raise your child not Hannah Montana's. Besides, from the looks of it, I don't think you want Hannah Montana (Miley Cyrus) raising your children anyway.

It's no secret that we are losing essential quality time with friends and family because of the time we spend in front of the tube. Our televisions continuously pour out immorality, violence and illicit sex; which is dangerous because we are prone to live our lives vicariously through what we see on TV. The commercials are usually only about thirty seconds long, so imagine what your favorite TV shows can promote in the time you spend watching them. The filth that pours into our living rooms through our TV is not limited to expensive satellite or cable packages either, it pours right through our antennas. The sexual content that is aired on TV is getting a lot bolder, resulting in more and more allusions of sexual intercourse being aired.

Pornography is literally creeping into our favorite TV shows. They show just enough sexual content for us to tolerate, and eventually we end up accepting it as the norm. What once made us feel awkward and uncomfortable to the point where we blushed, now makes us feel indifferent. Have you taken the time to notice how ubiquitous pornography is? It is available to whoever, whenever. The only way young adults use to get their hand on porn; was when they were snooping around in the attic, or under their parents' bed. Now, all they have to do is turn on the family comput-

er; begin surfing the net, and that dirty monster will be star-
ring them right in the face. The evil spirit of pornography
has found a way to turn our homes into a brothel, pressuring
us into buying sex. There is an unlimited supply of porn on
the internet. Everywhere you turn there is a pop up of a
beautiful girl, that says, click here for a good time. Pornography uses sexy men and women to exploit our weakness,
causing us to become addicted to sex. Pornography portrays
a distorted view of our sexuality. It turns people into objects
of lust. It separates sex from love and emotions. It treats sex
as if it is a hobby, recreational activity or some type of sport.
It teaches us to deny our morals and indulge in immediate
gratification, making us equivalent to the likes of wild ani-
mals. Pornography implies that sex has no rules or bounda-
ries and that any and everything goes. Once pornography is
viewed, it opens the door to be able to view it in your mind,
allowing your imagination to run away, imagining things
you wouldn't ordinarily imagine. Your constant random
sexual thoughts and fantasies leave you feeling guilty and
often ashamed. Pornography will mold your sexual behavior; what was once unthinkable like, sodomy, masochism,
and orgies; become desires that we long to fulfill. Pornography is anti-family because it encourages adultery which
leads to divorce. It encourages pre-marital sex which leads
to teen pregnancies, illegitimate child births, and single parent homes. We live in an eroticized society but pornography
is one of those unselective evils that we can all do without.
We should also do without some of the music and video
games that entertains us. About ten years ago, if you
would've asked me can movies, music and video games be a
bad influence on kids I would've told you no, and I would
have been wrong.

The video games kids play now aren't like playing Pac-
man or Super Mario brothers. Games are much different

now. There is a video game where the whole object is to commit crimes without getting caught by the police. I mean, you can literally car jack citizens by dragging them out their car, beat them to death with a bat, and take off in their car. Throughout the entire game, you commit crimes like this over and over. Now, I use to say that you can't blame a video game because some disturbed child goes out and takes a life. Well that is no longer my stance. Although, I believe video games aren't solely the blame, I believe they play a vital role. When an immature child plays a video game that should only be played by a mature adult, the consequences can be very damaging. The kid who plays first person shooter games along with the rest of the games that endorses criminal actively and violence; they become desensitized to violence and the quality of human life. They began living their lives vicariously through the game; and overtime become corrupted and their way of thinking becomes irrational. When denied something as simple as a ride to the mall; a reasonable response from them might be to; drag someone out of their car, beat them with a bat, and take off in their car. After repeating a crime like this over and over in their head all day; they finally turn what was supposed to be a video game into reality. Now there is no way you can blame a situation like that entirely on video games, but at the end of the day it has an influence.

Music is a good influence when it's the kind of music that speaks life into a person. Unfortunately, we don't always listen to good music. We like to listen to music that speaks death into us. I always listened to rap music that I felt related to me. The kind of rap music that highlighted my life style and painted a picture of all my struggles. I opened my ears to rap music that glorified, selling drugs, using drugs, premarital sex, multiple sex partners, material things and a criminal way of living. From my juvenile years, well into my adult years, I was brainwashed by this music because it implanted unfruitful thoughts in my mind. It had me content with living the same futureless life. It convinced me that the only way I could make it out of poverty was to sell drugs. It instilled in my mind that women were bitches, and whores who are objects to be used for sex. The music made me feel that if I didn't have designer clothes, fancy cars and bling-bling, then I was a nobody. Don't get me wrong, all rap music isn't like this but this is the particular type of rap music that I liked to bathe in; it's what helped me self-destruct. Instead of the music building me up, it broke me down. It never inspired or encouraged me to do better. It never motivated me to be a business owner or to go to school. It didn't encourage me to be a loyal man and honorable father. The music made me feel as if there was no hope for me, which gave me the justification for my rebellious actions. The music was responsible for planting seeds of falsehood in my head; because there was plenty of hope for me. I had plenty of opportunities. There is a million ways to get out of poverty besides selling drugs. Women are not bitches and whores they are queens and should be treated accordingly. There is so much more to life than empty cars and bling-bling. The music that entertained my soul was equivalent to two devils on both sides of my shoulders screaming in both ears. The music took advantage of the fact that I was a teen who was resisting any form of lawful or parental authority and capitalized on it. I listened to sinister music for so long my mind became hardened to ever thinking that the music was affecting me. To guard against being brainwashed by all the filth the toxic music pours out. Reverse the damage by listening to music that speaks life into your ears; not music that speaks death; robs children of their innocence strips people of their morals and causes affliction to the soul. If this type of music is listened to for a prolonged period, it can leave its victims brain washed. You should also be careful not to let society trick you into believing music played over the radio isn't harmful because it's the so-called radio version. Yeah, they may bleep out words or dress them up, but it's not the words, it's the meaning behind the actual words. Besides, if I were to take a pig and dress it up by putting a suit and tie on it, will it still be a pig? Thank-you, my point exactly. It is what it is. You can't lean on society to make decisions for you. You must take the initiative to prevent corrupt messages from entering your soul and take extra precautions to protect our youth, because it's obvious society could care less. Our number one goal should be to protect our children's innocent eyes and ears, from seeing and hearing any form of malicious content. If you have already failed at that miserably, like I have, you should put some preventative measures in place to prevent further damage and entertain their very souls with inspirational material.

In many ways, entertainment reminds me of driving through traffic in the city of Chicago. It can be an enjoyable experience when traffic is flowing smoothly but get stuck in traffic, and it can become a very unpleasant one. Oh, you don't understand what I'm talking about? Well let me explain. Every time I travel through Chicago, I get caught up in all the scenery around me. I see the skyline of the city and it captivates me. I become taken aback at how tall the Willis Tower is. I love finding and pointing out the John Hancock building or the Four Presidential Towers. It amazes me how calm and peaceful Lake Michigan is leading up to the busy and complex city. I always find myself awe-struck staring at the huge Ferris wheel the closer I get to Navy Pier. These land marks are sights you must see while driving through the city; but there is much more that goes on while traveling through the city. Let me try to paint you a visual. Let's say you are driving past the Chicago Tribune building, heading

toward the Water Tower building and traveling along the
side of you, there is a couple in a minivan cursing and
fighting and on the other side of you there is a man in a
wheel chair with a sign that says, "I'm Hungry". Pretend
you are passing Soldier Field, heading toward the Museum
of Science and Industry and you witness a semi-truck run a
guy over on a motorcycle. You look at the corner of Madi-
son and Pulaski and you observe illegal street vendors selling merchandise; and you witness someone get pick-
pocketed. Under the viaduct at Lake Street; you spot a couple of hookers soliciting their services who look no more
than fifteen years old. If you decide to roll by Wrigley Field
after a Cubs win; you can see a group of drunk fans singing
the victorious, "Go Cubs Go, song". Cruise down I-94 and
you will see a billboard that says, Erotica Encounters, Next
Right, Poker and Black Jack, Fourteen Miles ahead. Traveling through the high volume of traffic in the windy city can
be very fun and entertaining. However, you can be easily led
to places you had no plans on going, seeing things you had
no plans on seeing. The constant stop and go of traffic can
really test your patience and become very frustrating. This is
what I mean when I say entertainment reminds me of driving through Chicago's traffic, because at times, I find myself
stuck in traffic in my own home; seeing things I had no
plans on seeing and going places I had no plans on going.
What may have started as me googling what time the next
show starts; turns into me viewing highlights of last night
basketball games, watching a video of police brutality, comparing my phone to the latest iPhone, ordering something
that I don't need, filling out a survey for a free gift card that
I will never receive and ashamedly, looking at some form of
pornographic material. By the time I'm done, I've forgotten
what I went online for to begin with. In this day and time, it
is very easily for us to be stuck in an entertainment traffic

jam because of our desire to stay connected to the social media and other various forms of entertainment. We can't do anything without receiving notifications and other frivolous messages on our social devices without feeling we have to respond to them. I witnessed the D.A. at my criminal trial correspond to text messages and emails on her phone the whole time she was prosecuting me. Everything we see and hear is entertainment for the soul. If our eyes are the windows to the soul, our ears are the gateway. It's important that we be extremely cautious when deciding what forms of entertainment, we allow through those entrances. Entertainment is like a good and bad friend who come to your home to keep you company. When good friends come over, they help lift your spirits up. They are a joy to be around, they give you good advice and comfort you in time of need. They also tell you about yourself when you aren't doing what you should be doing which makes you not want to be around them at times because you know they are right. On the other hand, bad friends may seem like they are fun to be around but deep down you know they are a bad influence to your soul. Their lies and deceitful ways convinces you to let them in your home, around your family and they act like they never want to leave. When they finally do leave, you find out they stole valuable belongings. We can't stop all company from coming over whether good or bad. However, we can put the proper security system in place to return bad company to the streets where they belong.

People also have this big notion that everything they see on the internet and TV; or read in magazines and newspapers, or hear on the radio is deemed true. Well, it is so not. Half of what you read and hear is a bunch of crap. People say and write made up stuff or tell you half of the truth for attention or some type of personal or political gain. Do your best not to be deceived by false information. When you find a good source that gives accurate information and helps better you; that is the source you should stay connected to.

Beware of the hidden evils in the world. Watch what kind of company you let hang around your soul because we tend to act out what we see and hear. Occupy yourself with more positive things. Since you are reading this self-help book, you are already headed down the right path. Understand that just because our government makes it legal, doesn't make it morally right. Stand firm and keep your integrity in check. Of course, we can't isolate ourselves from everything our souls disagree with. Therefore, I'm not telling you to go around changing people's radio stations and criticizing everyone for what they watch on TV. I'm also not telling you to ball up into the fetal position with your eyes closed, covering your ears with your hands every time you are around something you don't care to see or hear. I'm not even telling you not to watch or listen to things that you don't morally agree with. All I'm telling you to do is be careful and know what you are dealing with because it's so easy to become molded into the worlds mold and what a wicked mold that is. If you are watching and listening to things that you will feel uncomfortable sharing with friends and family or even a stranger because you are ashamed, I'm going to have to say that you should detach yourself from it. If you are shamed of something, it is obvious you feel it is wrong. Many of us don't have the slightest idea why we act the way we act, but the truth is we act out what we see and hear. On that note, I'm going to leave you with this little bit of advice.

"You think you got to do and act better, when really all you need to do is see and hear better." (Take heed.)

EXERCISE

❧

You have been working on your summer body for three years now, when are you supposed to be finished? You mean to tell me you still haven't worn that swimsuit you bought a while back? You haven't gotten in shape yet? Hurry up, what are you waiting for? I'll admit, it was cute when you first gained five pounds, but twenty-five pounds? That swimsuit should be the least of your worries now. You should concentrate on your health. How long do you expect that body of yours to hold up? Slowly but surely, you have been breaking that body of yours down. You have been adding extra pounds to that frame every year. How many diseases and chronic illnesses do you already have; and how many are you trying to put yourself on the market for? You can say you need help all you want, but, it's impossible to help you if you won't help yourself. Exercise is something you know you should do, and why you should do it, and yet you don't. Instead of pushing your luck and limit, try pushing yourself. It all starts with you. You must take the initiative to get off the couch and then the extra initiative to exercise.

Excuses, excuses, excuses. All that comes out of your mouth are excuses. You claim to have all these problems but all you have is excuses. All excuses do, is tell you, you can't when you can and hold you back from achieving your goals and dreams. You have ninety-nine excuses and a result ain't one. The reason there are no results is because excuses don't net results. If you make excuses, you will never get a result.

You say, "I don't have time." I'm sure you can find time between surfing the web and watching TV. Really? You should be honest with yourself and say, I don't have time for that.

"I'm too exhausted." Exercise helps the body get better circulation which gives you more energy.

"My back hurts, I got bad knees, my shoulders ache." Exercising in a pool takes the pressure off your joints.

"I don't like getting sweaty and smelly." Put some deodorant on and exercise in the air conditioning or shade.

"I got a head ache, my feet hurt, my show is coming on."

Enough of the excuses. The only time you should give an excuse is when you pass gas and politely say, excuse me. When you and your ex were together, you didn't make all those excuses. You two should try hooking back up. Besides your ex; always made you happy and feel better about yourself. Never gave up on you even when you gave up on you. Knows all of your weaknesses and will help you strengthen them. Was breath taking but at the same time helped you breathe again. The truth is, you and your ex look good together. Don't you remember all of the compliments you received when you and your ex were together? Of course I'm talking about (Ex)ercise, who did you think I was talking about? It's time for you to get married to Exercise. As you can already see, excuses have gotten you nowhere. Aren't you tired of those lame excuses? Make a commitment to exercise for the rest of your life. Exercise is precious to your body. Look at all the benefits. It strengthens muscles, bones and your immune system. Exercise reduces the risk of heart disease, diabetes and cancer. Helps your lungs take in more oxygen. Stress and anger is stored in the body and exercise relieves it, causing you to feel happier and stress free. Exercise preserves the body. It causes you to use up calories in exchange for a flatter tummy. With proper dieting of course. Your muscles love to work and exercise is what works them. Exercise makes us better role models to those who look up to us. Exercise makes your skin look clearer and you healthier. That truth alone should make you want exercise back in your life. Incorporating exercise into your life is not at all impossible. Especially if you have it very high up on your priority list. I'm only telling you because I have experienced life without exercise. Every time I strayed away from exercise, slowly but surely, I'd start to feel the side effects. I become easily prone to pulling a muscle and catching muscle cramps, while I watch my muscles deteriorate to mush. I catch shortness of breath and frequently become fatigued. My once solid six pack transforms into a two liter and after sometime depression starts to settle in my body. I'll spend weeks talking about, starting back exercising next week. I would always make an excuse about not having the time or energy to exercise. I'd eventually start back exercising until I got distracted. I'd go from working out all the time, to some of the time, to none of the time. For most of my life, exercise and I have had an on-and-off type of relationship. I knew life without exercise was bad for my body. That's why I committed to making exercise a part of my life for the rest of my life. I no longer let anything or anyone get in my way. After years of being inconsistent with exercising, I finally made the decision to make it a priority and it turned out to be one of the most beneficial decisions of my life. Here's how and why I came to that decision. I had to be at work by

4:00 a.m. and I worked ten to twelve hour days. Believe me, I found plenty of excuses not to exercise. There was only one gym open at that time of morning and it was on the other side of town. It was too far and too much of a hassle for me to even want to get there. Truthfully, it was just too early for me. There could have been a gym right next door to my house and I still wouldn't have gone because I did not want to get up any earlier than I already had to. After work, I found everything besides exercising to occupy my time. Whether it be Junior Jujitsu practice, helping baby girl with her homework, cooking dinner or watching my Chicago Bulls game. I made an excuse. I either didn't feel like it or I was too tired to even think about working out. I always planned to go home after work to shower, eat, relax for a second then go get a workout in at the gym. After relaxing a minute, my workout got pushed off for tomorrow. It was as if my home had some sort of powerful spell over me. As soon as I made it home and took off my shoes, all of my energy escaped right through my feet. The couch was like some sort of hard workers trap, because every time I sat down on it, I couldn't get back up. I couldn't move. After my body convinced my mind how tired it was, my mind would convince my body to get some rest today and exercise tomorrow. My mind should have been honest with my body and replaced tomorrow with never. It should have said get some rest today and exercise never. Because that's what always seemed to happen. Over and over, I let that couch of mine get the best of me. I kid you not, the only exercise I got was walking back and forth from the couch to the refrigerator, to the bathroom, and eventually to bed. Every single day I did not exercise, I felt guilty about it. I knew I was not doing right by my body. I decided to make a stand. No longer was I going to neglect what my body needed today for tomorrow. I turned tomorrow into today. Exercising became a priority in my life. The new order given strictly to my body from my mind was, after work go directly to the gym. Don't go home, don't stop at the store, don't go pay bills. Go directly to the gym. Working out at the gym became as important as working at my place of employment. No longer did I schedule appointments based on the time I left work but based on the time I left the gym. I dedicated one hour a day, six days a week to taking care of my body. Of course, I don't expect you to do the same. I am very much aware that some of you haven't worked out in years, if ever at all. Every one's goal should be to exercise forty minutes a day, three days a week. If you find that to be too much of a commitment, start at twenty minutes a day, three days a week. Those figures should get you in the ballpark and they are based on my own personal experience. I usually don't go longer than six months without working out. It is too easy for my body to get back in the habit of not working out. Which means the bare minimum of twenty minutes a day, three days a week may be too much for your body. Please don't feel discouraged. Do what you can. Something is better than nothing. Start off as small as you like. You can start with as little as four minutes a day. If you were to work out four minutes a day, three days a week. By adding two minutes each week you will improve to twenty minutes in as little as two months. All you have to do is start. There are going to be plenty of days when the body doesn't have energy or doesn't feel like working out but showing up is what counts. Show up now and you will be showing out later. Never do more than your body can handle. Actually, do a lot less than what you can actually do and build yourself up from there. Here is a perfect example. If you know you can do twenty-five sit-ups, start out doing ten and gradually increase it from there. The reason I say this is because your body may be able to do it, but it also has to recover from doing it. Believe me, it is not a good feeling to wake up and find out your body is sore and stiff to where it's too painful to move. That's no good. Do yourself a favor and slowly add time, then reps and then intensity. You will also find out that you can't actually do what you think you can. I go through this, every time I return back to the gym. My mind will tell my body to warm up before the actual workout. My mind remembers the warm up routine I was doing six months ago, one hundred jumping jacks, fifty pushups, fifty situps, fifty body squats, andjog in place for two minutes. Each exercise is supposed to be performed right after the other. My body attempts it. It does a hundred jumping jacks and gives up about a quarter of the way through the push-ups. My body can't finish because it is in pain, gasping for air. What once was a warm up, now is an extreme workout and my body doesn't want any parts of it. One time after being away from the gym for a while then returning. I convinced myself that I was going to squat three hundred and fifteen pounds, ten times like the good ol' days. Well I only squatted it once and it caused my body to scream, "Are you out of your mind!"

This over ambitious attitude caused me to hurt my lower back and strain a muscle in my butt. I almost had to take a leave of absence from work. For this reason, I strongly suggest starting off slowly and easing your way into it. Starting slow also helps build confidence. Listen to your body. It will let you know what it can and can't do. It's okay to push yourself but don't beat yourself up. You don't want to discourage yourself to the point where you give up. I rather see you give your all. Giving it your all means giving it everything you got except up. Never give up under any circumstances. Once you have taken the first step by doing it. Take the next step and that's don't quit doing it. If you are doing it by yourself, it is okay to have some help or a motivator.

Recruit a friend to exercise with you. It's easy to miss a day at the gym when it's just you, but it is hard to hold a friend up at the gym. I strongly recommend trying out a certified personal trainer. We all need that someone or something from time to time. If you don't have a support group already create one. You can add anyone you like: friend, family, coworkers; however, make sure they are only bringing positive energy to your group. Keep all those negative dream killers far away from your group. Let them talk behind your back all they want, that's what got them back there in the first place. Don't let those people who say you can't and won't hold you up. Believe me, they know you can and will and they are terrified of it. Set goals for yourself and share them with your support group. They will support you every step of the way, cheer you on, and help you meet your goals. Go to social media and join fitness groups. They always post interesting stuff about the best supplements, food, and all kinds of fun and exciting workouts you can do. That way, whenever you find yourself bored scrolling down your news feed, you can get some excitement and optimism about exercising from random posts. Working out does not have to be boring either. There is more to it than bench presses, ellipticals and treadmills. Do stuff you love doing and change it up often. Play basketball, go ice skating, dancing or hiking. Get creative, invite your support group over to play tag or dodgeball. Don't want to work out at a gym? I don't see anything wrong with exercising at home. Try one of those workouts on DVD. How about watching your favorite TV show while jumping rope or riding a stationary bike? Go for walks around your neighborhood or go sightseeing with others. Think safe and be careful. Stay on roads and paths that frequent many pedestrians. Create a fitness world around yourself. Read fitness magazines, place motivational banners on your walls, computers and your wallpaper on your phone. Get into complete character by wearing the proper athletic apparel. You are now an athletic personal trainer. Well maybe not, but there is nothing wrong with acting like one.

You don't need to be a professional athlete to be athletic. You can't run as fast as Usain Bolt but you can run faster than you do now. You can't jump higher than LeBron James, but you can jump higher than you do now. Stay motivated. Put the "work" in "workout." Don't let anything or anyone hold you back.

"If you can't fly then run, if you can't run then walk, if you can't walk then crawl, but whatever you do you got to keep moving forward."

Martin Luther King Junior

Take care of your body because it is the only home you have to live in. It's your brain means of transportation. Your body is there to protect you and keep you alive until the inevitable comes. It would be in your best interest to make your stay in your body a comfortable and enjoyable one. Give it the proper care that it needs. Your body is there to serve you and it will take care of you as long as you take great care of it. As soon as you stop caring, so does your body. You are the body's leader; it is your responsibility to discipline your body correctly. Our bodies have their own unique limits but all have the same basic necessities. You can't keep a body awake forever, eventually it's going to get some rest. When the body needs to relieve itself, it's going to whether you like it or not. Give the body constant attention by grooming, and conditioning it. Feed it all the proper foods and make sure it gets the proper amount of rest. Don't neglect the body because the body is essential to your well-being. If you deprive or overwork the body, it will give up on you. Train your body to have good habits. You may be easily tempted and influenced by others, but your body is only influenced by you. The goal is to have optimum health by proper nutrition, adequate rest, and physical exercise. However, most of us compromise our health by taking the unnecessary risks, by experimenting with drugs, alcohol, unprotected casual sex, junk foods, lack of exercising, and many other risks that could cause permanent damage. If your body is in bad condition, don't just give up on it. Get it in order. Your life depends on it. You can accept conditions for the way they are or you can be responsible for changing them. Your future is determined by what you do today, not tomorrow. Think of your body as you would a child that needs good parenting, and become that parent. Your body is going to want to eat junk food all day. Your body is not going to want to exercise, it would rather sit on the couch and watch reality shows all day. It will rather take a nap versus doing some work. It may say no when it should and yes when it shouldn't. This is where you, the "good parent" come in at. Your body may throw all type of tantrums and fits along the way but make sure that body of yours eat balanced meals, get an adequate amount of exercise and rest. Relieved is what the body will feel when it doesn't have to fight against all those harmful bad habits.

You don't need a doctor to tell you to eat right and exercise. Listen to your body. Every pain you feel is your body crying out for help. It's saying enough of the fast food, walk me, stretch me, please no more pie, help me! Build that body of yours up. It's not easy. It's not a walk in the park it's more like a hundred of walks in the park. It won't happen overnight but it will happen with dedication and hard work. Don't let what you can't do interfere with what you can. It's not going to happen all at once, but boy once it happens. It's similar to a flight of stairs. You don't jump all of the stairs at once, you go up one step at a time. What are you waiting for? Stop staring up those steps and start stepping up those stairs! Impose your will over your body, because a well put together body is the best outfit you will ever wear.

FOOD

ৡ৽৵

Truly, there are many people addicted to drugs, alcohol, sex, nicotine, gambling and many other things. On the contrary, what about food? Food is causing the world to be overweight. Food is killing people all over the world, especially in the United States. I've never really had a problem with food, but I have witnessed many people who have I see a lot of the same similarities with being addicted to food as I do many other addictions. Overweight people tend to develop depression, anxiety, mood disorders and low self-esteem. This can lead to increased suicidal thoughts. Does that sound familiar? Those are some of the same problems associated with other addictions. People develop an unwarranted dependency on food like all other addictions. Some people try to find any excuse they can to eat food when food is just a nutritious substance. However, to some, food is love, comfort and joy. I always wonder why people don't stop eating the foods that make them overweight as soon as they start to see themselves gaining weight. Well, that's easy for me to say because I'm not addicted to food. The same group of people might have wanted to ask me, Why don't you stop drinking as soon as you start to feel a buzz off alcohol? or

Why do you drink until you are sloppy drunk? Also, prior to you judging, the same group of people might want to ask you, Why don't you just say no to drugs; why don't you just quit smoking cigarettes; why do you consistently bite your nails if you want them to grow long: or how about, why do you still text while driving and you know it is against the law. You see, many overweight people have tried to diet and many other things. However, they have failed many times at their attempt to break their addiction. Likewise, many of us have the same problems. There is just something about the phone vibration to notify you of a text alert that makes you check it while driving. Even though you will be out of the car in ten minutes. There is something about the drag of a cigarette that won't let you quit smoking. Even though no one likes the smell and it messes with your lungs and causes cancer. Before we judge, we should look at ourselves in the mirror first. A high priest once said something like this, "Why do you look at the speck of sawdust in your brothers' eye and pay no attention to the fifty-foot telephone pole in your own eye?"

How can you say to your brother, let me take the speck of sawdust out of your eye, when all the time you have a fifty-foot telephone pole hanging out of your eye? You hypocrite! First take the pole out of your own eye and then you will see clearly to remove the speck from your brothers' eye! We all may have different addictions, but we all have the same problem. We have become slaves to the body. Some of our bodies love food more than it should. After reading this chapter, you will begin to see food for what it is. It is not your friend or companion; it is just simply fuel for the body.

Nutritional foods, examples being fruits and vegetables help our bodies in many ways. They promote stronger immune systems, stronger bones, and healthier looking skin. Nutritional foods help prevent common colds, diabetes, cancer, and many other diseases. Junk foods cause many of us to be overweight. Which is why running around with the kids is out of the question. It is the cause to our knee and back pain. If you are not overweight and eat nothing but cakes and other processed foods, it doesn't necessarily mean you are healthy. Most will develop visceral fat which is fat that stores around your organs and puts you at risk of things like a heart attack. The fat keeps you out of breath often. We all have witnessed a skinny guy whose body is flabby.

I was probably about ten years old when I was watching the news on TV and they were showing how three foreign exchange students from Africa were adapting to living in the United States. I will never forget how the news reporter said the students had never eaten potato chips. As a ten-year-old boy, that was just unbelievable to me. I couldn't even imagine to not have ever eaten potato chips. I've seen babies without teeth eat potato chips and here this news reporter was showing these foreign exchange students trying potato chips for the first time. Two of the students struggled to get the chips down while one student spits out the potato chips after trying them. It was as if someone put sand in their mouths. The look on those student's faces was priceless. They looked as if someone had played a sick prank on them. I remember wondering to myself, why did the African students react like that to a good ol' bag of potato chips? The answer to that question did not come to me until years later. In fact, it took me doing time in the county jail for me to understand, why. I had done time before, but this particular time was different. Normally I had outside support from loved ones. They supported me by accepting my collect calls, writing letters, visiting, and sending me money, so I could buy canteen. The jail was required to give us three meals a day, but canteen was common hygiene and food products that the jail sold at an extremely high price. If you have ever been to jail or know someone who has, you would know that the food they serve in jail is awful. They don't use salt or any type of seasonings to satisfy a human taste bud. They literally turn hospital food into gourmet food. You never knew what you were eating for most meals. It is usually a tray of slop that they happily call chow. I never ate slop when they served it. I would always eat the desert which was usually a cake or a cookie, then give or throw the rest of the tray away. I always ate a jailhouse brick instead. Which consisted of chips and noodles crumbled up like bread crumbs and usually some type of meat like beef jerky. You add hot water, form it into a brick, let it sit for five minutes and, voila! You have a jail house brick. It sounded nasty to me also, but after eating slop, I was willing to try anything. The brick actually turned out to be pretty good. This particular jail time I had to do without any outside support. I had no one. I was lonely and broke. That meant that I had to eat whatever the jail provided me with. It was eat slop or starve, and I wasn't going to starve. They fed us every day at the same times. Breakfast at 7:00 a.m., lunch at 11:00 a.m., and dinner at 3:00 p.m. There was a sixteen-hour time period that passed between dinner and the next meal. I usually ate the dessert and picked through the slop. At night, my stomach would start talking to me. I was often so hungry, I couldn't sleep. After about two weeks, I was forcing myself to eat the whole tray. My stomach was starting to get satisfied every night. As the weeks went on, my taste buds became numb and I got accustomed to eating food with no flavor. I was able to eat all the slop on my tray. If they put a rubber boot on my tray, I would have ate it. I even started trading my dessert for a whole tray of slop. I wanted the slop to get in my belly just as bad as Fat Bastard wanted Mini Me in his. I didn't care as long as I got full and was able to sleep at night. Don't get me wrong. I couldn't wait to get home and eat some real food. My mouth use to water every time I saw a fast food commercial. Words like savory, juicy and succulent always caught my attention. All I could think of was *Foooooood!* (in my Homer Simpson voice).

More than half a year had passed, and I was finally being released from jail. When most people get released from jail, they can't wait to be with family, kids, significant other, friends, have sex, do their drug of choice and eat a good meal. The only thing I cared about was eating a good meal. My first stop was the Pizza House. A local spot that serves the best pizza in the world and even better Italian Beef sandwiches. I ordered my Italian Beef with mozzarella cheese, banana peppers and a cup of au juice to go. After waiting for fifteen minutes with my stomach turning in knots from the smell of pizza and other foods; my sandwich finally arrived in a grease stained brown bag. I made it home to the kitchen table; and took my sandwich out to of the now ripped bag from all the grease. After unwrapping all the white parchment paper from the sandwich, I dipped the sandwich in the cup of au juice and took my first big bite. Boy was it good! My taste buds were delighted from all of the good flavor and I let them enjoy every minute of it. About as fast as my taste buds became delighted, they also became fatigued from all of the sodium. My taste buds sent an instant message to my brain stating that this sandwich is entirely too salty. My brain responded back by saying maybe the au juice is salty and not the sandwich. So I took a bite without dipping it in the au juice. I got the same results, entirely too salty. I forced myself to swallow it down when I really wanted to spit it out. There was no way I was going to finish that sandwich. I thought my favorite place to eat Italian Beefs had lost their touch. Over time, I realized it was not them, it was me. Everything I ate was either salty, sweet or too spicy. I ate home fried chicken, it was salty and too spicy. I ate a Big Mac from McDonalds it was good but the pickles had to come off because they were too salty. I ate a pepperoni pizza; it was good once I took off the salty pepperonis. I made my favorite Kool Aid which consisted of: two packets of orange and one package of pink lemonade and two cups of sugar. I mixed it altogether with water and put the Kool Aid on ice. Once I started drinking the Kool Aid, it literally tasted like I was pouring liquid diabetes down my throat. My drug of choice was alcohol. I bought my favorite hard liquor, Hennessy, only to find out that it was too sweet. I did not like the taste of Hennessy anymore. I had to find another drink to satisfy my addiction. How could this be? How could all the foods and drinks not agree with my taste buds anymore? Then the answer became obvious. All the time I spent in jail without eating much salt and sugar actually brought my taste buds back to life. They were far from numb, because before I needed to add a lot of salt to my food, now I needed only a little bit of salt if any. You see, over time, our taste buds become numb from all the foods that are saturated with sodium and sugar to such an extent that we need a lot of it to make our food taste better. When your taste buds aren't numb, foods taste better the way they naturally are. You don't need a piece of cake or chocolate to satisfy a sweet tooth. All you need is a piece of fruit. Fruit is naturally sweet and good for you. I must say, the maker of fruit is a perfectionist. Which brings me back to the foreign exchange students from Africa. They were used to eating foods that were natural, not processed, created by a perfectionist to nurture the body. Their taste buds were not numb like mine were from all the over use of salt and sugar. So when they tasted a thinly sliced fried potato loaded with sodium for the first time. It was like poison entering their mouths. They spit out the potato chips because it did not taste like the foods they were accustomed to. They were accustomed to natural unprocessed foods.

What our bodies need is nutrients. Nutrients act like fuel to the body to provide us with energy. One reason obesity is on the rise is because processed foods have been on the rise. When foods are being processed, they are being loaded with food additives to change the look and taste. Processed foods provide your body with most of the stuff you should say away from like: sugar, sodium, saturated fat and refined carbohydrates. The stuff that's in processed foods is what I like to call junk food and it's best to stay away from junk foods because it doesn't do your body any good. The three African foreign exchange students never ate processed foods. They ate to survive. They ate food that provided their bodies with energy to complete daily task. They ate foods so their bodies will function properly. Unlike many of us Americans. We choose the food that we eat because of the way it tastes and looks not because of what it can do for the body. If we did we would not eat all of the junk foods that we eat knowing that they slow us down, rot out our teeth and cause health problems. As a child, I remember my mother telling me I couldn't drink my pop until I finish eating all my dinner. I'm sorry, I'm from the Chicago land area and I cannot call pop, soda, for the life of me. My mother did not want me to get full off pop without getting full off of real food. This was her reason for telling me I couldn't drink my pop first. She always told me not to eat anymore candy or I couldn't have cake until I had eaten dinner. I thought she was being spiteful, because who cares if I get full off pop, the goal was to get full wasn't it? My mother also use to buy me and my baby sister Cheerios for breakfast instead of our favorites, Lucky Charms, Frosted Flakes, Captain Crunch and Fruity Pebbles. I thought that was just evil. All of those good varieties of cereal and far too often we were stuck with Cheerios that needed sugar that we didn't have available. You never heard a commercial say Cheerios were gr-r-reat or magically delicious! Everybody went cuckoo for Cocoa Puffs, not Cheerios. I believed my mother bought Cheerios to punish me and my baby sister. As I got older, I realized my mother wasn't trying to punish us, she was actually trying to give her children healthier food options. She didn't want me to be full off pop because it had no nutritional value. She wanted me to be full off foods with essential nourishments for the body. She wanted her child to be full off what she called, real foods. My mother knew that Cheerios would provide her children with the proper nutrition other than cereal loaded with sugar. Which brings me to this conclusion: why did I even know what non nutritional foods taste like? The exact same way everyone else knows what junk food taste like. Our family and friends and the endless forms of advertisement like billboards, commercial, marketing and all the different types of junk foods.

When my daughter was born, I wanted the best for her. I did not want my daughter to become a picky eater, I wanted her to like real food. There is nothing worse than trying to feed a hungry person who dislikes most foods. My goal was to keep my daughter from being that person. In my attempt to avoid it; I tried to keep junk foods away from my daughter. I explained this to family and friends and everyone agreed that it was a great idea. However, early on they made it evident that they cared nothing about helping me execute it. Every time I looked up, my daughter was tasting some form of junk food. Whether it was a lick of her cousins Blow Pop, or a finger full of frosting off her aunties cake, or a spoonful of her mother's ice cream, she was always tasting something. My daughter never did get a chance to get accustomed to eating foods provided by a perfectionist. So therefore, her reaction was totally different than the African foreign exchange students when tasting junk food. She had a look of satisfaction on her face. She would literally drool everywhere and on everything with a smile on her face from ear to ear. The first time she held her head up was when she was in the living room playing on the carpet with one of her Leapfrog toys. I came out of the kitchen and sat on the couch in the living room by my daughter with a plate of apple pie right out the oven. As soon as she smelled my apple pie, she stopped everything she was doing, sat straight up and was reckless eyeballing my plate. The first time my daughter walked was when she was six months old. I came home from work to find my daughter standing up, holding on to the living room table eating an ice-cream cone her mother gave her. My daughter looked up at me with a smile on her face waiting for me to pick her up and give her a hug. I was happy to see my daughter also, but, I was disappointed that she was eating an ice-cream cone. I was forced to look like the bad guy again because there was no way I was going to allow my daughter to eat the ice-cream cone. I walked to my daughter leaned down gave her a hug and she gave me a wet kiss like always because she kissed with her mouth open. I told my daughter I love her and that she couldn't have any more ice-cream. I grabbed the ice cream cone and walked to the other side of the room. My daughter started screaming hysterically at the top of her lungs. She had hurt and wronged written all over her face. My heart hurt looking at my daughter in this state because I knew she did not understand. When I looked at my daughter again, I put a smile on my face because my daughter was doing something remarkable. I realized that while my daughter was crying hysterically. She had let go of the table that she was using to hold herself up. She was so mad at me that she didn't realize she was walking. She was taking steps towards me. My baby girls' will was bringing her to get her ice cream back.

She made it five steps short of her goal before she fell. It didn't matter though, because I made up the difference. I picked up my daughter, gave her a big hug, kissed her on the cheek and said "Da-Da loves you. I'm sorry baby."

I also gave in and gave my daughter back the ice cream cone that she was so determined to get back. I was in the state of shock. I just witnessed my daughter walk for the first time. A six month old? Yeah it was an amazing moment. Before my daughter was even one years old, she already was being controlled by food. If I would have gotten on my hands and knees and said come to daddy, walk to daddy baby, trust me, she wouldn't have come. My daughter always found a way to get what she wanted especially junk food. There have been numerous times when I've dropped my daughter off at her grandmother's house for a while' and told her grandmother don't give her any junk food. Only to come back to my daughter licking a lollipop as big as her head. I mean, really? Why do people feel they have to give children junk food? In our world today, people feed their dogs, foods, based on the way they look and smell. Not because it is the best thing for their dogs' health, but because it looks better. I have been guilty of giving children junk foods also. The only legitimate answer I can give as to why that is, is that it was a learned behavior. I learned that you give children junk food as a reward and also you can gain favor from a child by giving them junk food. I know now that you can give a better reward like fruit as a treat and it will be of a mental value as well as a nutritional value to the child. Equaling two positives. Versus a mental and non-nutritional value equaling a positive and a negative.

As you see, many of us are hooked on junk foods before we even have a chance to make a decision. We as parents, need not to introduce our children to all of these toxic junk foods. You have to want the best for your children in the long run.

The best advice I can give you is to never even start your child off eating junk food. Don't even give them a chance to crave cakes and candies. Let their taste buds be virgins to foods that are processed like the African students. If it has to go through any process leave it up to nature. Like the honey bees. No toddler will turn down the natural sweetness of honey. If we prevent our children from eating processed food, they will never develop a physical craving for them. So, look for healthier alternatives.

For those of us who love to indulge in all the junk foods. We need to eat the foods that provide our bodies with what it needs and not what it wants. We need to just say no to processed foods. I know you are probably saying that's easier said than done, but trust me it is possible. One way to gain control is too fast. When I did time in jail, I was forced to fast. The jail didn't put much if any salt or sugar in the food. Those circumstances helped me gain back control of my taste buds. You can do the same also, and of course I don't mean going to jail. You can gain back control without getting rid of junk foods completely. I'm not saying don't ever eat cake again or bacon that's packed with saturated fat and sodium. What I'm saying, is don't let your body eat whatever it wants whenever it wants. Our bodies are childish in a sense. If you give a child as much candy as they want, they will eat until they have a stomach ache or vomit. Our bodies will do the same also. Our bodies will eat junk food until we are obese with back and knee aches and shortness of breaths. Many people think of fasting as just a religious practice. Well, I'm here to tell you that anyone can fast. Fasting is when you tell your body it can't have something like food, sex or alcohol. It's strictly restricting your body from whatever your will doesn't want it to have. You may do it often without even knowing it. I know many people who say they only drink alcohol on weekends, or one cup of coffee per day. No eating before going to bed. There are many different restrictions you can put on your body. With the few examples I provided; you can see that they were not complete restrictions. They were simply restrictions to prevent too much consumption of something. When you fast, you are just sacrificing for the body. You can try things like instead of using five packets of ketchup as usual on your fries, just use one. Instead of using ten packs of sugar in your coffee use five. Instead of using butter, sugar, or salt on your bowl of oatmeal, eat it plain. Make a sacrifice for your body. We all have heard or said this phrase, "You might not understand now but you will when you get older." Let your will tell your body that. You may lose flavor, but you gain better health and life style. Let your will become the responsible adult and make good choices for your body. You can say, eat a plain bowl of oatmeal or oatmeal with strawberries? You can tell your body you will treat it to the dessert of its choice every Sunday. Just make sure your will is in control. Sometimes, I will fast and not let my body take in food for a few days. The reason for this type of fast is to let my body know who's in control. A war always breaks out between my will and my body. While fasting my, body keeps begging for food and my will keeps saying no. I must admit, my first attempt at fasting like this for twenty-four hours, my body won. Over time, my will got stronger and started winning the war. If I do a three day fast, my body will fight for two days but on the third, it puts up no fight at all. When I'm done fasting, my body doesn't even crave fast food or any of the other junk foods. All my body wants are some nourishments to restore its energy. After fasting, my body doesn't complain or argue about anything when it comes down to food. It is more than grateful to eat a bowl of plain oatmeal. By fasting, I train my body into subjection. My body develops respect for food, versus being spoiled by food. When you fast, you also give your digestive system a break from the nonstop work it has been doing since the day you were born. During this time, you should also do some form of body cleanse and get rid of the toxins in your body. By doing this, you will rejuvenate your body. Toxins slow the body down. They make our organs work harder than need be, because they are trying to eliminate the toxins from the body. I recommend doing at least a two-day cleanse. It makes my body feel like new and it gives me the energy that I have been missing. I no longer feel sluggish and tired all the time. Foods, drugs, alcohol, cigarettes, and hygiene products like deodorant, lotion and body sprays and eating processed foods are some of the ways toxins enter the body. We should eat more fruits and vegetables because they provide antioxidants to help the body fight off the poisonous toxins.

I also found out that it is a lot easier to deny your body junk foods when you do not have them around to tempt the body. Most of our wills are not strong enough to abstain from the junk foods if they are around to tempt our bodies. It is best to not have them around us at all. Eliminate all the junk food from your home. Clean out the refrigerator, cabinets, pantry and yes, your sock and office drawer. Where ever you have junk foods get rid of it. You are less likely to be tempted and lose a battle to the body. Remember, the body is like a child. Children can't sneak cookies out of the cookie jar if there are no cookies in the jar to begin with. Replace junk food with healthier food and your household will more than likely snack on healthier snacks when hungry. Please don't believe the hype. All healthy food is not delicious. I have seen many infomercials where they put something like a banana, apple and spinach in a juicer and turn it into juice and say the juice taste good. I even watched an infomercial where someone put a whole orange, pineapple, and banana in a juicer, peel and all and say, "It tastes good." Are you kidding me? That stuff is disgusting. I always wonder how much the guest got paid to take a sip of the juice, put a smile on their face and then lie to all the viewers by saying, "Mmm… that tastes delicious." Because I say, "Eel… that crap is gross! Drinking your food like this is called juicing. Not steroid juicing but the actual juice from fruits and vegetables. Juicing is very beneficial for the body because it allows your body to enjoy 99 percent or more of the nutrients versus when you cook them. Juicing is like drugs in a cup without the side effects. I like the recipes for juicing that use only fruit or a high fruit, low vegetable mixture. I dislike the recipes that call for the dark leafy greens and I especially dislike any recipe that calls for the peel also. In my personal opinion, some recipes for juicing taste good, most taste bad. If you don't know, let me be the first to tell you that all healthy foods will not taste good. Trust me, my taste buds dislike a lot of healthy foods that I eat, yet I still consume them. Remember this, food is a nutritious substance consumed by humans to maintain life.

I understand my body needs the proper nutrition to maintain a healthy life, so I eat and drink many health foods regardless of my taste buds' approval. Have you ever taken a shot of hard liquor? No one really cares for the taste. All we really care about, is if it is smooth enough for us to get it down, and if it will give us the buzz we are looking for. Or how about cold medicine? Many of us will take whatever medicine we can take that doesn't make us vomit, to make the body feel better. Speaking of cold medicines, we can prevent many colds if we take in the proper nutrition. The proper nutrition gives our bodies what it needs to fight viruses and things like the common cold. Many of our problems come from lack of the proper nutrition. Our bodies develop vitamin deficiencies due to not eating a diet consisting of foods that provide us with the proper nutrition. This is why, I eat a lot of healthy food my taste buds dislike. I eat food based on what my body needs and not what my taste buds wants. For instance, when I'm done working out, I consume foods with carbs and protein because that's what my body needs to help repair my muscles. When I feel a cold coming on, I eat foods with a lot of vitamin C because that's what my body needs to help my body fight off viruses. In the winter months, I drink a lot more milk to provide my body with vitamin D that is usually provided to me by the sun in the summer months.

We must take good care of our bodies. Don't let your body march all over your will and eat whatever it wants. Provide your body with what your will wants it to have. whenever you allow the body to have a certain food or drink, make sure the body knows that your will allowed it. The next time you are eating food, think about why you are eating that particular food and how that food is benefiting your body. If your answers are something like: I'm bored, just because, or I don't know. You need to get your body in check and fast. Don't let cupcakes and Twinkies control you. Remember all food is, is fuel for the body. Provide your body with the proper fuel and it will always appreciate you. Stay faithful to your body and your body will be faithful to you. Provide your body with what it needs and your body will be there for you when you need it most. Take care of your body. Impose your will.

MIND

❦

Do you know what it feels like to be a prisoner of your own mind? We always hear about someone being out of their mind, but what about the people that are being held captive by their own minds? There are individuals that are confined to the space between their skulls. They become their own worst enemies because this causes them to defeat themselves. As a prisoner of the mind, you continually tell yourself what you are incapable of doing. You tell yourself that you can't do something so often that you begin to believe it. You become so convinced that you are inadequate that you don't even put forth effort to accomplish anything. Your mind then begins to feed off this daily hot garbage. The results of this mindset is that you never consume the foods that nurture, make grow or help the mind mature. Too often for entertainment, you force yourself to watch all of your memories that are the most troubling to your psyche. You constantly watch years and years of footage of all your failures. You catch mini-clips of various disasters that have occurred in your life. You've watched every episode that suggests why it won't work along with the endless highlight reels of disappointments broadcasting all the things you've done wrong in your life. These images you watch over and over in your mind reiterates "why" you think you can't do things. Your whole thought process is botched. You overthink and overanalyze every episode from your past. No matter what's going on or how good some things may seem, you tend to take the worst viewpoint expecting the worst outcome. All of your views and expectations are based off the motion pictures you've replayed in your head. You can't begin to think clearly when you are bombarded with a steady stream of poisonous thoughts due to the foul litera-ture, random nonsense, and the other assortment of filth you've surrounded yourself in. You have trapped yourself inside your own mind rotting away like a prisoner in captiv-ity.

Food for thought. A thought is just that, a thought, noth-ing else. They'll come and go as the wind. Your thoughts travel through your mind as if they are on an endless con-veyor belt. Your thoughts are generated from your surround-ings and the things you feed your mind, yet they are random and uncontrolled. If you surround yourself with filth, you will have a lot of filthy thoughts. Likewise, if you surround yourself in positive things you will produce positive thoughts. No matter what, it is inevitable that you will have thoughts that are both welcomed or unwelcomed. Some thoughts will make you sit back and wonder, *Where on earth did that come from?* Some thoughts that flow through your head will have you wondering are you weird or insane. Take this example for instance: When I'm driving on the road and some idiotic motorist decides to cut me off. I have had thoughts of chasing them down and running them off the road. I would see myself walking up to the driver's win-dow, punching it out, then pulling the driver out the win-dow. I can see myself bashing his face in until he falls to the ground. Once on the ground, I envision myself stomping him until he's floating in and out of consciousness, slashing all the tires on the car, taking the keys out the ignition and telling the driver, "Now you know what it's like to almost lose your life," right before shoving the keys down his throat.

I've also had thoughts about putting my foot knee deep up every young man I see sagging their pants while walking in front of me. Luckily these are just *thoughts* that I let pass through without entertaining, as I can only imagine what kind of trouble I would be in if I actually acted on it. There is no problem if you entertain wholesome or fruitful thoughts, however, unwholesome thoughts become an obstacle when you do not allow them to pass through and decide to entertain those wretched thoughts. Now you are doing what is known as thinking. Thinking is a beautiful thing when it's constructive but for some reason, people choose to think about all the wrong things.

Many of us have what is known as stinking thinking. We choose to nurse all of our negative thoughts. Random thoughts run through our minds rapidly:

I make the best gumbo on the planet.
I take pretty good care of my family.
My neighbors are hardworking people.
I don't think they like me at work.
They never invite me to parties.
My boss never says good job.

As soon as the negative thought, *I don't think they like me at work...* popped in our head, we started to entertain it. We let all the wholesome thoughts pass and yet refuse to let the negative ones through. Instead, we began adding to the thought. Worse, once we start thinking negative thoughts, we eventually start to construct them as truth. We start believing our negative thoughts until they become inevitable. I want you to take a moment and dissect this saying, "You are not at all what you think you are, but what you think, you are."

At first, I found this statement to be contradicting until I diligently analyzed it. After examining it in depth, a light bulb popped in my head and the saying started to make sense. I decided that if you think you are a bad person, the saying is letting you know that you are not at all a bad person, rather you have allowed your negative thoughts about yourself tell you that you are.

The dangers of our thoughts are that they can very easily turn into actions. For this reason, it is imperative that you control that in which you think about. Use your mental energy on things that produce good fruit. Think of bad thoughts as seeds that can grow up to be poisonous weeds that will choke and smother fruitful plants. The only way these bad seeds can grow is if they receive special attention from you. When you constantly think of negative unfruitful thoughts, your mind begins to water the seed. The more you nurture bad thoughts, the more water you add. If you don't gain control of your thoughts, you are nurturing the innocent seeds that will turn into a full grown batch of poisonous weeds.

When a married man lusts after women he has actually committed adultery by the actions of his mind. One of our presidents, Bill Clinton, was impeached because of what began as a lustful thought, he eventually acted on. You must continually deter your mind from unfruitful thoughts. In order to do so, you need to be conscious of the things you see and hear. Don't indulge in things with poisonous content. Instead watch and listen to content that will make you a better person. This is important in both your entertainment selections and personal relationships as well. For instance, if you have a friend and all they like to do is reveal all of their poisonous thoughts to you, respectfully let them know that you are uprooting all of the poisonous weeds you already have in your garden and that you would appreciate them if they would help you not spread anymore bad seeds. When you see and hear more positive things, better thoughts will come to mind. When good thoughts come to mind, treat them as good seeds. Take control and give these seeds the proper nourishment and watch them produce good fruit. At all costs, keep the weeds out of your garden.

You are not at all what you think you are. You are not what others think you are. You are what you think others think you are. This is an extreme way of thinking because you are assuming what others think about you. Half the time they don't even think, what *you* think they think, about you. I've run into people with this manner of thinking many times. I'm quite sure you know exactly what I'm talking about. After a breakup, a guy will say of their ex-girlfriend something along the lines of, "She was just a gold digger," or "She didn't want to sleep with me, she just wanted to sleep with my car." I've also witnessed beautiful women who are disliked by almost everyone they come in contact with. They tell me they are disliked because everyone is jealous of them and their good looks. Truthfully everyone dislikes them because they act like a B.I.T.C.H. Point, blank, period.

You should give little care and attention to what other people think about you. What you think about you is far more valuable. If all you do is think about all the things that are wrong about you, you need to make some serious changes in your life. Give yourself more good to think about. You should accept that everyone you meet will not necessarily like you. I once overheard a guy say he didn't like Tim Tebow because he thought he was gay. I asked him why he thought that and his reply was, "Because he can have any girl he wants and he's always talking that God stuff." That just goes to show you that people will have false opinions of you for all the wrong reasons and there is nothing you can do about it. I personally admire Tebow for those very same reasons that someone else thinks is a negative attribute. I will certainly assure you that if you have a better opinion of yourself, the majority of the people you encounter will also. After all, people don't make you or break you. You make or break you. Stop accusing people in your head of thoughts they didn't think. These are your thoughts that you cast off on others. I mean really, who do you think you are to give someone else an opinion of you?

During part of my childhood I was the only boy in the home with my mother and younger sister. Although I was two years older, she was one of those baby sisters who would let you know in a minute that I was in no way the boss of her. She would waste no time showing you every reason why she was in fact the boss of me (and everybody else). I was by most definitions, a typical boy and did what young boys did. I ate what young boys ate, talked how they talked, played how they played and slept how they slept. I wasn't the kind of boy who played with Barbie dolls, except when I was cutting the heads off. My mother and sister picked on me about everything. I could never seem to do anything right in their eyes. All they ever said was, "You do things like a boy." I mean they nagged and complained about everything I did.

"Why do you hold your fork like you are going to stab somebody with it?"

"How do you not know that you have ketchup on your forehead?"

These were the type of exchanges that I went through on a daily basis. As a result, I really thought something was wrong with me. I thought everyone thought I was useless, worthless, the scum of the earth. I could never figure out how my sister could play outside and have as much fun as I did: running through the same parks and climbing the same trees without getting her clothes and shoes dirty. After playing, I looked as if I had been rolling around in a pig pin. They rode me so hard about everything that I convinced myself that I was an inept misfit. I was convinced that everyone thought I was an out of place, deranged child growing up. I can remember me doing things that my mother thought was crazy but in my mind, I felt I was being very clever. I could never forget the look on my mother's face when she walked in the kitchen and stumbled upon me drinking Kool-Aid out of what she called a cereal bowl designated solely for cereal. All she could muster up to say to me was, "Why?"

Before I could finish explaining my rationale, that I had grabbed the bowl because it was closest to me; and I was too lazy to reach behind the bowls to get a cup, she had already walked out the kitchen. Who said these little bowls were for cereal only anyway? My mother would also throw her hands up in submission every time she witnessed me do things like eat my green beans with my hands. She would rant and rave about how I'm supposed to use one of the forks that she bought for that very purpose. Where is the rule that says you can't eat green beans with your hands? Thank-you, my point, exactly. Besides, I found it a lot easier using my trusty hands versus a fork. All the dirty looks and constant bickering at me reiterated why I thought I was out of place growing up. It made me think that everyone thought I was crazy.

This is such an important issue to me that it caused my mother and I to get into a big argument during my adult life. It all started over string cheese. My seven-year-old son was in the process of opening up a stick of string cheese when my mother decided to intervene. She barked at him in a condescending tone, "Why are you trying to open the string cheese with your teeth? That's why they have a peel here

sign on it." She grabbed the string cheese from him and proceeded to show him where the peel here sign was. The scene
was all too familiar to me. It shook me right back to my
childhood. I felt that I had to protect my son from growing
up thinking he was an inept, misfit like me. So I immediately snapped at my mother.

"My son can open his string cheese however he wants. If
he wants to open it with his teeth he can open it with his
teeth. Besides, I use my teeth. It's a lot easier using your
teeth versus trying to peel where it tells you to. Because
most of the time it doesn't even feel like it's supposed to. If
you want to peel yours where it tells you to go right ahead.
But my son can open his string cheese, however he likes."

My son was stuck in the middle looking confused as he
watched his dad and his G-Ma argue back and forth over
string cheese. I know that all my mother was trying to do
was help out and teach my son how to follow instructions;
but what she failed to do was let my son know that he had
options. Instead, she made it seem as if it was a wrong way
to open it. I couldn't begin to tell you how many times I
tried to: peel here, or tear here, or poke here only to become
frustrated. I'm almost sure that whoever manufactured the
Capri Sun container was playing some kind of sick prank
because I swear they bullet proofed the, *Poke Here* indenta-
tion. I've torn up every straw known to man trying to poke
through what was apparently a brick wall with a plastic
straw. If the straw did manage to go through: it pierced
through the whole container causing me to lose most of the
juice.

Convincing myself as a child that I was crazy, I met this
thought half way. I gave up trying to do things their or anybody else's way. I just didn't care anymore. After becoming
an adult and taking a thorough examination of myself, I realized that I'm not crazy, and others didn't think that about me

either. They just have a different way of thinking than I did. I was not at all perceived the way I thought people perceived me. In fact, many people considered me as a nice, intelligent young man. I asked myself, "Why am I running around acting crazy?"

I spent a bulk of my childhood *thinking* that I'm inadequate because I was worried about things that didn't even matter. I was so unsure and uncertain of myself that I just gave up on a lot of things- things that actually mattered all due to my irresponsible thinking. Never again would I let any thought make me think that I'm inadequate because of the way I decide to do things.

I later took the time to explain to my son to never think that he was crazy because he did or thought differently than someone else. I wanted him to know that he should learn easier more efficient ways to do things, but in the end, after weighing the risks and the rewards, he should do what's best for him. I can't believe we were actually arguing about how to open string cheese. String cheese opening should never become a big dilemma. Concern yourself with things that actually matter.

An important thought to keep in mind: *IT IS OKAY TO DO THINGS DIFFERENTLY.*

If you have been trying to do something and it hasn't been working, it is okay to try and do it another way. Be open minded and willing to embrace new advice. There is no guarantee that all will be good, but some will be worth a try. You are never too old to learn something new. You also are never too old to learn something stupid. Be open to doing things differently, but not to open that your brains fall out. With that being said, I'll tip my glass, or should I say cereal bowl that I still drink out of from time to time.

Don't ever be in the opinion that you have to live up to the reputation that has been given to you. Far too many peo-

ple in today's world think they have their so called good or
bad rep to live up to. It all starts with something they heard
somebody say about them, then they try to be exactly that.
We see it all the time. For example, say you compliment
someone telling them that they always keep a clean house. I
assure you every time they know you are visiting they will
make sure that their house is clean. There's also those flat-
tering compliments. You tell someone, They always wear
the finest clothing and they will spend the rest of their life in
debt trying to dress in the crème de la crème. Those individuals who gained a reputation of being a loser spend the rest
of their life in debt trying to prove it. Stop with all the she-
nanigans. You will feel a lot freer when you don't think you
have to impress somebody trying to live up to a reputation.
You will be relieved of the burden of proving that nasty reputation to be true. Don't Rep-U-Tation, Rep-U. If you haven't been representing yourself well, now is the time. I
know you have done some things that you are ashamed of,
but those things don't represent *you*. Don't for one second
think that you have to accept a reputation. If you think you
are worthless, I want you to think again. If you think you
have to impress everyone, well think again. I want you to
think hard and long until you finally realize that you are a
great person. You are not perfect. You make mistakes, but
you move on to being a better you. Your light will shine
bright when you represent yourself accurately, that's what I
think.

Memories can play a vital role in our mind. Imagine if
every time you wore a red shirt you got sick. We know the
colors we wear have nothing to do with us getting sick but it
would be pretty hard to convince you of that. You would
stay far away from wearing anything close to red. When we
are stuck with a whole bunch of bad memories, it is hard for
us to be optimistic about anything. We think that everything

is going to turn into a catastrophe because we have been through and witnessed far too many to think otherwise. It's really hard to feel success is a possible outcome in any situation, when you have seen nothing but failure after failure and have been let down your whole life. Even when things are going your way in the back of your mind you think it's just a matter of time before tragedy strikes. When you are constantly betrayed, taken advantage of, stripped of things you have worked hard for and left to fend for yourself. You will almost certainly think the world is against you.

People always wonder why you act the way you act but they would never know unless they take a walk in your shoes. You can't change your past so don't even bother trying. The reason you have many of those bad memories is because you were surrounded by a lot of toxic trash. Some of it you may have actually created yourself. Nevertheless, the end result is a lot of trashy memories. It's not about where you're from, but, where you're going. I can assure you of this: if you are surrounded by toxic trash, you will be boxed in with some of the same trashy memories, headed down the same filthy road, reeking of the same toxic junk. You have to eliminate all of the toxic garbage from your life. It may include certain people like a friend or family member, or something toxic that you partake in like drugs of infidelity. If the environment you live in is a domestic waste site, move to an unpolluted area. Trust me there are greener pastures. When you are around better people, and doing better things in a better environment, it's inevitable that you will have fonder memories. You should never try to suppress your bad memories. You can end up causing more harm than good. When a bad memory occurs. You should acknowledge it as a bad memory then move on. Let it come and go. Don't hold on to it. With better things happening in your life you will have better memories. These new found memories will allow you to be more optimistic. Your actions will change and you will perform better. You will pick up more confidence and start to think I can and I will instead of the infamous I can't.

Stand firm and safe guard your mind. Some people spend most of their time grooming their hair, ironing their clothes keeping their nails well-manicured and making sure their home and car stays clean. All while neglecting their minds because they constantly let it feast on hot garbage. Everything you feed on this earth grows, including your mind. It's okay to feed your mind a little junk food as long as you have a balanced diet of educational and spiritual material to go along with it. Everything we allow our minds to absorb causes us to think of things along those lines. Our minds tend to ponder over the material we received. This is major because we serve our thoughts. When we are thinking about all the wrong things it means we are serving all the wrong things. I recommend following Paul's' advice that he wrote in his letter to the Colossians. Paul wrote, *"Whatever is true, whatever is noble, whatever is right, whatever is pure, whatever is lovely, whatever is admirable, if there is any excellent or praiseworthy, think about such things.* Philippians 4:8-9 If you allow your mind to indulge on these things you will have a very productive and fruitful train of thoughts.

From time to time our minds malfunction. They get rusty and in need of a major tune up. Our minds tend to get off track and travel down the wrong road, and get fixated on all the wrong things. This is sure to happen with the various forms of peer pressure going on in the world. This is completely normal but I will tell you a way to keep It from being a common occurrence. Renew your mind every morning. You ought to reset your mind as you would a watch that falls a few minutes behind every so often. One of the first things you should do every morning is have a meeting with yourself. Every morning after I have finished washing my face. I say, "self" myself says," hmm. Today is going to be an awesome day. We are going to make the best of this day by working hard, showing love to others, all while keeping a smile on our face and not worrying about things that don't matter. Whatever I have been lacking at, or spending too much unnecessary time doing: I let myself know that it's time to get back in order and what I specifically need to do.

I got to start back spending more time with the kids.

I got to cut out majority of the time I've been spending in front of the TV.

It's time to start back giving one-hundred in ten percent in my workouts.

I must work on being more sensitive to the needs of others.

Every morning I have a meeting like this to get things back in the proper perspective. To make sure I'm on the right track to being the best person that I can be. Cheesy or not, I look in the mirror every day knowing that I'm looking at a pretty decent young man. Some of you are too hard on yourselves. Every time you mess up, the very first thing that comes out of your mouth is, "I'm stupid, or I'm a bad person," instead of, "That's not me, that's not the way that I am, I'm better than that."

I challenge all of you pessimistic thinkers to stop looking in the mirror at all your faults and the bad you have done and look deep into that mirror at all the good. After seeing all the good walk away from the mirror and know that you are an awesome person and go elaborate on it.

A mind is a terrible thing to waste. Your mind is your own personal computer with billions of files downloaded on it's hard drive. Your mind is your understanding, your memory and the way you perceive things. All of your resources on how to survive and fulfill tasks is embedded in the mind. The mind is so powerful, it allows you to escape, take vacations and explore worlds that can only be dreamed of through imagination. Your mind allows you to form your own personal views and opinions. It allows you to place judgment and consider things. Your mind is what entertains all your ideas and brings your dreams to life. Consequently, your mind is what keeps dreams from ever getting off the ground. Let go of all the pessimistic thoughts and memories too free your mind. You have the key to unlock all the chains that are holding you back and I suggest you use it if you ever want your dreams to become a reality.

MONEY
੭ৡৡৢ

"America! We've got our priorities fudged up!" In my Bernie Mac voice, may he rest in peace. Seriously, we will finance a $50,000 vehicle and we don't even own the house we live in. We will finance a $2,000 vacuum that we don't need and yet we will say it's too expensive to get Junior a private math tutor. We'd rather pay thirty bucks a week for the rest of our lives for an extravagant entertainment system than to get baby girl swimming lessons. I guess your reasoning behind this is if Baby Girl stays out of boats and away from water, she won't ever have to worry about swimming. After all, it's been working for you all this time, right? Makes a whole lot of sense.

How many times are we going to waste our money buying our children Christmas presents that they only show interest in on Christmas Day? Or birthday gifts that they only play with on their birthday? Why must we continue to waste money buying our babies designer clothes that they grow out of and only get to wear a couple of times? Besides, all they do is waste food and drinks on them while they drag them back and forth across the floor. What a waste.

Stop buying stuff you don't need and worse, things you are not going to use. We as consumers continually fall for the same things over and over again: Buying on impulse.

Some stranger knocks on your door and tells you he will clean one room of your carpet for free if you will be kind enough to watch him do it. You agree because it is just too good of a deal to pass up. He pulls out this vacuum that has all of these fancy components and compartments that reminds you of Megatron. The carpet cleaning guy begins vacuuming your carpet with this Megatron looking vacuum and after each passage he turns it off and shows you on a white pad exactly how much dirt he pulled out of your carpet. By the dirt being on a white pad it really makes it more embarrassing. Then Mr. Carpet Cleaner instructs you to pull out your vacuum and make one passage across the carpet. As you do, he follows right behind you with Megatron and shows you on that embarrassing white pad how much dirt your measly ol' vacuum left behind. As if your vacuum ever stood a chance against Megatron. After he shows you how filthy and worthless your house and vacuum are, Mr. Carpet Cleaner decides he wants to embarrass you further by asking for your permission to go into your bedroom and vacuum your mattress. However, you are confident that he will be impressed by how clean your bedroom is, including your mattress. Furthermore, you change your sheets every day and even sprinkle a little baby powder on them to give it that fresh baby scent. You consent to the carpet cleaners request and minutes later Megatron is gliding across your mattress. Mr. Carpet Clean turns it off and reveals what he pulled out of your mattress but only this time he uses a black pad. He gives you the results as Maury Povich would to an unsuspecting father on his talk show. He says when it comes to you keeping a clean mattress or not, and you say you do, Megatron determined that that was a lie. You are in disbelief as he shows you years and years of baby powder and dead skin he has vacuumed out of your mattress. Mr. Carpet Cleaner's use of the black pad made it look that more disgusting because of the way the grayish baby powder and dead skin contrast against it. To top that off Mr. Carpet Cleaner puts a sample of the powder and dead skin under a microscope. He then shows you something horrific-bugs that have been living in your mattress feasting off your dead skin. He calls them dust mites. At this point you are beyond grossed out to the highest of grosstivity. All you want to do is get rid of the bugs you have been sleeping with. You don't even want that infested mattress anymore. The guy that came into your home as a humble carpet cleaner miraculously transformed into a vicious salesman. He tells you how dust mites messes with your allergies and asthma. He educates you on how dust mites reproduce and lay eggs in your mattress. Then he informs you that they survive by eating your dead skin and defecating throughout your entire mattress. Then he tells you how you can save your family from this bug invasion by purchasing Megatron. He lets you know that "Megatron" normally sells for $3000, but since he knows you care about your family and because you have the same color goldfish as his mother-in-law, he will finance it to *you* for $2000, but only if you give him the pleasure of taking your measly ol' vacuum off your hands. You holler, "Sold!" Just like that you bought a vacuum that you didn't even know you were in the market for, because you bought on impulse. If you were to have given yourself at least twenty-four hours to think about it, chances are you would have talked some sense into yourself. Like you don't even have allergies, so how would dust mites even mess with them. The only time you have ever had a rash was when you came into contact with poison ivy. Your last visit with your doctor he said you were in great health. The only area of concern was the five pounds that you put on. Plus, you've made it this long without Megatron, why would you want to fix what isn't broke? You're already in debt; you couldn't possibly afford another bill. Your mind will say "Uh... sorry Mr. Salesman disguised as a carpet cleaner, the answer is No." All you have to do is take the time to think. Don't get caught up in buying things off impulse, stop and think about it. A salesman doesn't want you to think, they want you to buy.

Ever paid attention to those late night infomercials? Hurry up and place your order while supplies last. In most cases supplies last as long as they run the commercial. Which is for years in most cases. They offer the same deal; they just want you to feel like you don't have time to think by creating a sense of urgency.

Let's make a change. Instead of putting a $3,500 down payment on a car and paying $500 a month for a car note, you should buy a $3,500 car and pay yourself $500 a month.

Stop buying and start investing. It doesn't make sense to pay same day delivery on a package that you will never need. What does make sense is to spend your money on things that save and makes you money. A thirty dollar coffee pot can save you over three hundred and sixty dollars a year on coffee alone. If you are living check to check, you need to put your financial priorities in check. Get a grip on your finances and start by budgeting. Budgeting is as valuable to prospering financially as oxygen is to humans. You can't prosper without it. Make it your business to know where every red cent of your money is going. Have you ever stopped to ask yourself what happened to all of your money? Have you ever looked at your gross income amount for the year and wondered where the portion that didn't go to taxes end up? I have, and here is how you figure it all out: Write down *every* dollar that you spend for the next month.

If you pay the electric bill, write it down. If you go to the movies, write it down, popcorn included. If you give Junior a quarter to get a gumball out of the gumball machine, write it down. Keep track of every dime you spend. At the end of a month you might find yourself in shock when you find that you have donated a hundred and fifty dollars to the vending machine at work. Or that you have accumulated over a hundred dollars in ATM and overdraft fees. You may discover that you spend entirely too much money on things that you don't use: premium channels, magazine subscriptions, unused cell phone data, etc. Now ask yourself if this is how you want your money to be used and beware of luxuries disguised as necessities.

You can always watch television, movies, and internet at the public library. Remember, you invest money into the library as evident by the money taken out of each paycheck for taxes. In case you didn't know, watching television and getting a newspaper delivered to your home is a luxury. It is also possible that you might discover that you have more bills than income or that you are pretty close to it. Whatever the situation may be, you really need to sit down and evaluate it with your financial goals in mind. Once you have identified the areas where you waste money, and the areas where you don't need your money to go, it's time to eliminate them. Eliminating entails sacrifice. That cup of coffee that you get every morning is not a necessity. Your Saturday morning appointment at the nail salon, you can do without it and you know what you can do with those funky cigarettes. I really feel some kind of way about cigarettes and debt which is why I feel the need to express my feelings for myself and those who feel the same kind of way.

Now check me out America. I want you to understand me on this one. Cigarettes do absolutely nothing for you, trust me I know because I smoked more than half my life. With

that being said, anyone who smokes cigarettes it's their pre-
rogative to do so. However, it is not right of you to ask anyone to borrow or give you money and you smoke. Especially
welfare recipients. It doesn't feel good to know that I, a tax-
payer, contribute to putting food on your kid's table and I
have to sit back and watch you smoke cigarettes that I can't
afford. It doesn't feel good to loan you money for your electric bill knowing you could have had the money if you
would quit purchasing cigarettes. If you can afford to buy
cigarettes, you can afford to buy groceries. I mean think
about it. Cigarettes cost more than the hourly minimum
wage in most parts of the country. Most people who smoke
cigarettes, smoke a pack a day, therefore the cigarettes they
smoke weekly is equivalent to the pay of a minimum wagers
full work day. That is literally over two in a half months of
hard labor spent on cigarettes. Why should anyone be forced
to pay taxes with their hard earned money to support your
smoking habit? It seems to me like you don't need any type
of financial assistance. I mean think about it America and
when you do that will begin the process of progress.

Okay, now that I have vented for myself and everyone
else let me get back to this thing called budgeting. In order
to get out of debt and gain financial freedom, you have to
give up and put on hold those things that you love, especially those things that cause more harm than good. If you *really* feel that you can't give them up at least cut back. For example, turn ten cases of soda a month into five. Your bills
should only be 50 percent of your household's income. 25
percent should go to savings, investments, and emergencies.
The other 25 percent of your income goes directly to your
pocket to spend as you like and I strongly recommend that
upon receiving your check you should pay yourself first. 25
percent of your earnings should go directly to your pocket
before even bothering with the bills, because you are the one

who really deserves it. The problem most of us have with this (25/25/50) Formula is that our bills are around 100 percent of our income and in some cases more. Which leaves us with no pocket or savings money. In these situations, you have to humble yourself and live a lot more frugal. You have to look at ways to downsize. Examples may be, getting a smaller house or apartment. It will also be a good idea to consider asking for a raise or getting a second job. Even if it means cutting your neighbor's lawn, at this point, any additional income will help. You have to do what you have to do and that is doing what is best. Continuing down the same path is only going to make matters worse. Let me say this again, "Humble yourself." If you want to recover from the financial disaster you have been through. You got to get into anti lazy mode and make some changes no matter how extreme they are. Even if it means going on a beans and rice every night type of diet. Begin by: doing your own nails, cutting your own grass, cook your own food, go fishing for dinner, bottle your own water, walk instead of drive and as much as I hate to say it, but if you are not going to quit smoking you can roll your own cigarettes for crying out loud. Starting a garden is a spectacular way to knock a large amount off your grocery bill. It doesn't make any sense to pay $2.49 per pound for tomatoes when you can grow them yourself.

Here is a quick review in the steps you should take to gain financial freedom:

Identify where your money is going.

Evaluate where you want your money to go.

Sacrifice by going without some of the things you love and eliminating all the things you waste your money on.

Budget by using the 25/25/50 percent formula.

Once you have accomplished these four things, you are on your way to accomplishing your financial goals. I really want you to impose your will over your finances, so here's a great tip. Pay this month's bills with last month's money. In other words, get a month ahead of your bills. This will prevent you from living paycheck to paycheck.

It has been said that money can't buy happiness. Well, I'd love to find out. Quick somebody give me a lump sum of money so I can get to the bottom of this. How on earth did money get such a bad name? They say money is the root of all evil. I mean really, money the root of all evil? They say, more money, more problems. A little more problems would be miniature compared to the problems I already have. They say you discover who your real friends are when you are broke versus having money. I can totally live with that. They say money can't buy love or friends. Who actually needed someone to tell them that? As a matter of fact, who is they? Who is behind giving money this bad name? Oh I see. They are the ones who worship money. They are the ones who made money their god. They are the ones who would pull every little conniving trick for money. That's why they talk bad about money because they don't want us to have any of it. They try to deceive us into thinking that there is something wrong with money and we believe them due to all of the evil that we see around them.

I'm nobody's fool. I know there is nothing wrong with money. Money isn't the problem, the problem is their love for money. Money is not the root of all evil like they say it is. It's the love of money that is the root of all evil and who loves money. Nobody other than they. Don't bother yourself with listening to them because that's just what, "They" say.

There's also those foolish people in the world who will look you right in the eyes and say they don't want to be rich. They just want to be okay financially. Well, isn't that the right thing (dumbest thing ever) to say. "I don't want to be rich." Then they follow it up with dumb excuses:

"Money changes people."

"Money makes you forget where you come from."

Money doesn't change people, it gives a person more time and energy to express who they really are.

Let's talk in truth about what money really is. Money is time and energy that enables you to act and do things. Money is an influential force in this world that has the ability to open and close many doors. Money is currency that can provide food, shelter, a better education and environment for someone. Money is what funds the research for developing cures. Money is what gives people the opportunity to pursue their dreams. Money is neither good nor bad. Money is power. If you like giving and helping, money will give you the power to be more charitable and helpful. If you love to play with money, it will help you have more fun. Money will give a greedy person the ability to be more selfish. If you enjoy mistreating people, money will give you the manpower to be more abusive. A person who likes controlling and using people as tools, money will give you the power to be more manipulative. People have this misconception that if they were to become rich it will change their lives for the better but this isn't necessarily so. All money does is magnifies what is already in a person's heart. A person who comes into some money who distrust and is suspicious of everyone will not all of a sudden start to trust every time. In fact, he will do the complete opposite like turning everyone into a suspect and becoming more paranoid. Have you ever wondered how a poor person can become rich then lose everything just as fast as they gained it? It's because when they gained their fortune they were irresponsible and becoming rich didn't automatically make them responsible. All they really gained was more money to waste.

I find myself a little irritated whenever I hear someone say they have money problems. Believe me! You don't have a money problem. What you have is a "You" problem. How could you possibly say you have a problem with money when you have none? Money has done absolutely nothing to you. It's safe to say that we all have problems. Those of you who claim that you don't have a problem have the biggest problem. Majority of you will claim lack of money to be your biggest problem. Many believe that more money will let people know how great and successful they are. They expect money to do all the talking for them. The sad part about this is that when they do finally get their hands on money to do the talking for them all the money says is goodbye.

If we are not responsible financially, more income only means more expenses and debt accrued. Expenses and debt can come in the form of our family, friends and integrity. We tend to chase more money to take better care of our families and end up forever indebted to quality time owed to them. We began to look down on people because they can't eat at the same restaurants; go to the same venues and wear the same designer clothes. We trade in our friends for exclusive memberships, recognition and meaningless relationships. As you can see, money isn't evil it's the person behind the money who might be evil. An evil person wants more money because it gives them more power to carry out their evil ways. A good hearted person wants more money because it gives them more power to be a blessing to themselves and others.

A man's life doesn't consist in the abundance of his possessions. A man's life is about what he can contribute to it not take away from it.

Fancy cars, money and clothes does not make you better than the next man, they don't even qualify as a contribution to life.

People have let the power of money have control over them. All they think about is money. I find it very ironic how a president of the United states can die, be honored by being put on a dollar bill and come back to rule as a dictator in a democratic ran government. Money lovers allow every aspect of their lives to be dictated by these dead presidents. The only thing on their mind is money. They can never be satisfied with money because they always want more. They are forever trying to make more than the next man. People who are ruled by money don't care who they hurt or how they treat people along the way to obtaining money. They don't care about the family and friends they neglect. They are depleted of good morals. Money lovers have sold their souls to the devil. They have put prices on things that should be priceless. I hear all the time of a parent who spend their whole lives working extremely long hours to make enough money to buy their child what they never had: what other kids can only dream of. When all their child ever wanted was quality time with their mommy and daddy. I don't care how much of it you make, money can never replace time and loved ones. The more money you make, the more people will notice you and want to be around you, however this will not make them respect and love you. If you are one of these people who use money to gain synthetic love from people what do you think will happen when it's gone? Don't let money be the focal point of your life because money will steer you away from all the things that matter in life. It will make you forget how to treat people. You will forget how to have fun and appreciate the most important people in your life. You will miss out on some of the most cherished memories: like your child's first steps or your spouse burning thanksgiving dinner. Money and material things is not at all enjoyable when there is no one to enjoy it with. You are what you think, believe and do, not you are what you possess. If your heart isn't grateful you wouldn't respect what you possess anyway. To be honest with you, you don't even need more to be thankful for, you just need to be more thankful. Lose that attitude of how ain't nobody ever gave you anything. Open your eyes and look at all the gifts around you. It's a gift to be able to read this book. My ultimate gift to you is this advice: love the giver more than the gift and an abundance of gifts will be headed your way.

PROCRASTINATION

৯৯৫

Sometimes our body tell us what to do first thing in the morning. As soon as our day gets started, our bodies began barking orders. You tell yourself the night before, let me get to sleep by 11:00 p.m. That way, I'll get at least six hours of sleep before its time to go to work." You know it only takes a half hour to get ready and it's about a twenty-minute drive to work. You set the alarm to 5:30 am to give yourself sometime; to catch some of the morning news, stop and get some coffee, put some gas in the car, get a good parking spot, and show up before 7:00 shift starts. Well, you go to sleep and awake to an annoying buzzing sound. You realize it's the alarm clock. You squint your eyes to look at the clock and it says 5:30 a.m., just like you set it for. You make your move to get up and your body says, "No, wait! Let me get five more minutes of sleep." You look at the clock and it says 5:37 am. Your body says, "We have plenty of time to make it to work by 7:00 a.m." Immediately you agree with your body. *That's right we have plenty of time.* You hit the snooze button and dose off. At 5:44 a.m., you are disturbed again by the annoying buzzing sound. You immediately hit the snooze button because you remembered that you have plenty of time.

Beep! Beep! Beep! Beep!

You roll over irritated and look at the clock and it says 5:56 a.m. The stupid clock was supposed to go off at 5:51 a.m. but you didn't hear it. Now your body is just doing what it wants. It doesn't even let you know when the clock goes off. You realize you don't have time to watch the morning news; or stop to get some coffee or even fill up the gas tank in the car.

I've got just enough time to get ready and go to work and punch in by 7:00a.m, is what you tell yourself. You make up your mind to hit the off button on the clock and get up. As soon as you reach the off button, your body says, *wait, wait, please no, wait five more minutes. You don't have to take a shower because you took one right before bed last night. You don't need to sit and eat breakfast, you can grab some leftover pizza on the way out.* Just like that, you hit the snooze button. Not only has your body convinced you to hit the snooze button. It also has convinced you to not watch the news or stop to get some coffee. It has even talked you into cutting out the things you need to do, like eat a good breakfast and take a hot shower. Now you wake up to a sound that just won't stop nagging at you. The stupid alarm clock again. You glance up at it and jump out of bed. The stupid clock says 6:34 a.m. You can't believe it but you don't have time not to believe because you're running late for work. You rush to the bathroom to wash your face and brush your teeth. When you enter the bathroom the sight of the toilet makes your body have to pee. Just as you would a child you let it go potty and it takes forever. You grab your toothbrush and toothpaste out of the cabinet. You struggle to get the last of the toothpaste on your toothbrush. Hardly any comes out but it's got to do because there is no time to get the new one out of the closet. You brush your teeth with only enough toothpaste to spit twice. It makes you feel as if you didn't do anything. You wash your face with barely warm water. You are so much in a rush you grab the empty tube of toothpaste and place it back in the cabinet. You run to your room to get dressed. In the process of putting your shirt on, you have to button it over because you buttoned it wrong the first time. You notice your shirt could use a little ironing on the sleeves but there is no time. You have to make it to work. You glance at the clock and it reads 6:40a.m. You give yourself some encouragement by saying, *Come on. I can make it on time if I speed it up.* As you turn away from the clock it flips to 6:41a.m. which drains the little encouragement you just gained. You go to the mirror and brush your hair. While brushing your hair, you notice a stray hair under your chin that can be tweezed if you had more time. Obviously it won't happen, at least not before 7:00a.m. You walk around the bed and put on your shoes. You remember to put on your favorite fragrance that everyone at work loves. You spray it on, after retrieving it from the dresser. You also grab your wallet and grab your watch and put it on. You can't help but notice that the time on your watch says 6:53 a.m. You start to panic until you remember that your watch is ten minutes fast. You tell yourself that you still can make it if you leave right now. You make a mental checklist in your head of everything you need. *Don't forget your work I.D., work bag, and keys,* is what you tell yourself. As you walk to the front door, you go through the living room and grab your work bag and I.D. *Check, check.* You get to the front door and grab your keys, *check*, and you are out the door. You jump in your car, put the key in the ignition and start it right up. You throw the car in reverse and mash the gas. As your pulling out of the driveway, you look in the rearview mirror and slam on the brakes, while simultaneously hearing a loud honk. You were inches away from putting the trunk of your Camry through Mrs. Anderson from down the street, brand new Mercedes Benz, passenger door. You turn and catch the look on Mrs. Anderson face. Her facial expression looks as if saying, *What on earth are you trying to do to me?* You try to say I'm sorry, but the words never come out because she's a block away. You exhale and finish backing out the driveway. Once backed out, you throw your car in drive and you are on your way.

You are driving 60 mph in a 45mph zone. Which is unusually fast because your rule of thumb is to never drive more than 5 mph over the speed limit. You throw that rule right out the window to put forth effort to make it to work on time. You tell yourself, *I hope I don't get caught by all the lights, and please don't let the police stop me for speeding.* You approach the first light and to your luck, it's green. You fly right through it. You fly right through the second light. You are moving like the wind through traffic. You make it through the third and fourth light with no problems. Everything is going your way. You hit your right hand signal and make a right hand turn. You put a smile on your face because you have the road ahead of you all to yourself. You realize you are still doing 60mph and the speed limit had dropped down to 30mph, you ease up on the gas a little. You ride past Pizza Hut and you realize you did not grab the leftover pizza out of the refrigerator. You look up and there is a red light, you slow down until you come to a complete stop. You look at the clock in your car and It say's 6:54a.m. You feel a lot better because you made up for a lot of time. You know you are only five minutes away from work and that you can make it on time. You realize you haven't even paid attention to the Steve Harvey morning show that has been playing through the speakers. You have been too busy trying to make it to work on time. You say no right away. Your body doesn't even try to change your mind because it knows you mean business. You glance at the clock and it says 6:56 a.m. You look at the empty road ahead of you then at the red light. Out loud you tell the light to come on. Before you can finish, the light turns green. You put the pedal to the floor. As soon as you get in the intersection, a school bus turns right in front of you with flashing red lights and a sign sticking out with the letters S.T.O.P on it. Now you are stopped on a two-lane road with a bus you can't see around. You see on child walking like a prisoner in shackles to the bus. The child finally gets on the bus and you are still stopped for what seems like forever. Then you realize you got to wait for this slow poke to walk to the back and sit down. As you watch the stop sign being rolled back on the bus, you glance at the clock and it reads 6:59p.m. It finally hits you that it's a left turn signal. The big yellow bus slows down and makes the widest turn you have ever seen. Before you know it, you have open road ahead of you and you are going 40mph.You were so eager to go that you didn't even realize how close you came to clipping the back of the bus because you had your foot on the gas before the bus finished making its big yellow bus turn. You make it to the road where your place of employment resides and you make a left turn without even signaling. You look at the clock and it say's 7:03 a.m. You pull up to the entrance of your place of employment. You put on your left signal however you can't turn in because it's a busy two lane road. You wait for the oncoming traffic to clear. While you are waiting you see Eric turn into work, Eric is the clown at work who is on his way out the door because he's always absent or late, and here you are arriving after him. You finally pull into the parking lot. You notice that the gas light is on. You ignore it and drive all the way to the back of the parking lot. You park right next to Eric who is already in the building. You turn off the car, grab your workbag and I.D. You get out the car and close the door. You jog for what seems like a mile up to the door. You enter the premises and proceed to punch in. You punch your work number in and press enter. The clock reads 7:08 a.m. You turn to walk away and right as you do, your boss walks up and says, "You are late." You start to make a big story but your heart makes you tell the truth, "I got stuck behind a bus from hell. It stopped every four houses and the kids took forever to load on the bus."

Now that is the truth in a sense. However, if we back up to 5:30a.m. when the alarm was going off. We would see that if we would have just got up and started our day like we planned. We would have never been in this situation. We actually would have been a little early, but, no we did what our body wanted to do. Our body made us wake up later, not eat breakfast, not drink a cup of coffee, not watch the news, almost get in a car accident, get stuck behind a big yellow bus, show up to work late with the gas tank on empty without allowing us to take a shower or at least put on some deodorant to stop all the perspiring that is evident by the ring under our arms! The truth is our body made us procrastinate. We should have just told our boss. I'm sorry but my body made me do it.

Procrastination is the act of being lazy in seed form. When you habitually defer the actions of the will, the seed grows into laziness. Laziness is what stops many talented people from being all they can be. They talk-to-talk but never walk-to-walk. They always say things that sound good: I'm going to start a garden, I'm going back to school, or I'm going to take the dog for a walk and it never happens. Procrastinators never happen to make it happen. Procrastinators have good intentions but never intentionally do anything to the point where they become idle. All they do is watch what everyone else does. If this sounds like you, it is time for you to start doing. It's time for you to will yourself to the top. There's an old saying, "If there is a will, there is a way." Well, I tell you, if you follow your will, it will show you the way. What good is your will to you if you don't follow it. Don't let your body convince you to do things when it gets ready. Make those lazy bones do things when your will is ready.

Everything the body does is not a deliberate defiant act to your will. Sometimes it is carelessness and old habits. You have to break those old habits and replace them with good ones. Believe it or not, people were not born lazy. They actually had to practice at it. They actually had to practice procrastinating over and over until they became idle. In order to get up in the morning, the body has to be disciplined. You have to practice getting up every morning. You should not depend on an alarm clock to wake you up. My alarm clock didn't go off is not an acceptable excuse. I can recall times when I used the alarm clock as an excuse. I use to party all night and leave myself less than three hours of sleep before work. I would set the clock at 3:00a.m. in the morning for 6:00a.m. in the morning. Only to wake up at 10:00a.m. in the morning and realize that even though I set the clock for six in the morning, I forgot to turn the alarm on. Sometimes my excuse for not getting up on time was because I would set the alarm clock for 6:00 p.m. instead of 6:00 a.m. Sometimes I would wake up late because I didn't hear the alarm clock go off because the volume was turned all the way down. The reason It was turned down was because the morning before it awoke me under mental distress and the first thing I could reach was the volume to stop the annoying sound. I had turned the volume all the way down and forgot to turn it back up. Every time one of those moments occurred, I always blamed the clock and never myself. My childish body was content with depending on an alarm clock. Those childish ways kept me behind the ball; they made me miss out on great opportunities, they hindered me from being all I can be. In order for me to reach my full potential I had to train my body to do something as simple as get up in the morning. I made it a goal of mind to get up with the birds.

My starting point was making sure I got the proper rest at night. I still set the alarm clock to wake me up for insurance purposes. As soon as I heard the alarm clock go off, I forced myself to get right up. Over time, I started waking up well ahead of the alarm. Now my internal clock wakes me up before the sun every morning. I get up around five o'clock a.m. whether I'm going to work or not. With practice, my will muscle became stronger and overcame my body's bad habit of depending on an alarm clock every morning. When I find myself awake past one in the morning, my internal clock still makes sure I wake up before the sun. You see, I practiced waking up over and over again until it became second nature for me to wake up with the birds. When you practice, you expose your body to what you want to become. Set limits for your body and allow your body to operate with-in those limits. With practice, old behavior patterns can be changed and new ones learned. You might not achieve your goal right away but practice makes perfect. Many have fell while learning to ride a bicycle, but, with practice the act of riding a bike becomes second nature.

You were supposed to be here a half hour ago! Those were the irate words I heard often from my ex-girlfriend; when I would show up late to pick her up from work. I didn't show up late intentionally, I just had very little respect for time. She would always complain about how much she dislikes me showing up late and let me know how much of an inconsiderate person I was. I would always let her know how sorry I was and give her a whole bunch of excuses as to why I did not make it on time to pick her up from work. I must admit that she was right. I should have been more considerate; considering the fact that I didn't like when my ride home was always late to pick me up from work. I could never forget how much that made my blood boil. I remember when I was sixteen working in a shoe store at the mall. I had no problem getting to work, it was getting home that caused the problem. The mall closed at nine o'clock at night and there was no form of public transportation running at that hour. A friend who was also a coworker of mine had no problem bringing me home from work because he lived right by me. On the days I worked and he didn't. I had to find another ride home. I would often ask one of my friends or cousins to pick me up from work. After they take me through a whole ordeal of I don't have any gas in my car, and gas is over two dollars a gallon, and I don't have any money. They would normally agree if I gave them ten dollars for gas. They would probably ask me for a fortune now with today's gas prices. I remember working hard for the six hours that was on my schedule and feeling a sigh of relief when the last customer walked out the store. All I had to do once the last customer left was clean up the store and my shift was over. I always told my ride be there at 10:05 because even if I got done early. I couldn't clock out until 10:00 and it took me five minutes to walk to the mall entrance where my ride picks me up. I would feel so good when I put in a hard day of work and walk out those mall doors and my ride was there waiting on me. On the contrary, when I walked out those mall doors and wasn't able to see my ride, was one of the worst feelings. I remember it like it was yesterday. Me standing at the entrance waiting on my friend Brian to pick me up looking like a lost puppy. It seemed like every time I was in that situation, I did a lot of

talking to myself. The conversation would normally go like
this:

It's ten after ten, he better hurry up I'm starving.
I hope mom cooked something for dinner.
I should have brought my coat to work.
It's kind of cold tonight.
Look at the walk on that girl, I should get her number.
Eww... Her face looks like Dennis Rodman.
I'm glad I didn't approach her.
Where is my ride at?
It's 10:27 p.m.
I told him be here five minutes after ten.
There's a lot of people at the movie theater tonight.
Something good must be playing.
Ahh... Friday After Next, came out tonight.
I got to go see that.
It can't be better than the first?
They should have kept Chris Tucker in it.
Man, where is my ride?
That girl almost backed into that shopping cart.
Women can't drive for nothing in the world.
*I can't believe someone actually bought Kobe Bryant
shoes.*
I mean who wears Adidas?
It's 10:47p.m.
I hope he'd didn't go to entrance A instead of J.
Nah, he knows to come to J.
Maybe he thought I said five after eleven.
*I did tell him to pick me up five minutes after eleven a
couple of weeks ago.*
But that was just because we had inventory that week.
Yeah... maybe he thought I said five after eleven.
*I should have eaten that half a Cinnabon that Sarah of-
fered me.*

We must stop at Wendy's on the way home.
I should call and see if he left his house yet.
Nah, his mom will get mad if I call at this time of night.
It must be after eleven because my boss is heading to his car.
Yep Its 11:06.

My boss would always see me waiting on my ride and ask me if I need him to take me home. My pride would always force me to tell him, "No, my ride is on the way." This time he said he would wait on my ride just in case they didn't show up. I convinced him to leave: by telling him my ride is at the movie theater and the movie isn't over until a quarter after eleven. He said, "Since the movie will be letting out any minute; I guess I'll see you later and drove off."

Where is my ride at?
My fingers are getting numb
It's 11:12p.m.
I should have just gotten a ride from by boss
Everyone's starting to leave the theater
The parking lot is getting empty.
But then my ride might show up and I'm not there.
11:24p.m.
Wow!
There is only one car in the parking lot.
I'm not walking home.
I'll go hide in the mall before I walk.
I'll call the police to let them know it's past my curfew.
At least I could get warm in jail.
Whoever walks to that car, I'm gone force them to take me home.
What am I thinking?
I could have just got a ride from my boss.
Man, its 11:37p.m.
Why me?

If I had my own car I wouldn't be going through this.
I can't wait until I get my own car.
I'm not gon' give anybody a ride.
I wouldn't care if they needed a ride to their mother's funeral.
I promise, they will be walking to it.
Should have been here at 10:05 and it's 11:40.
I won't talk to Brian ever again.
I wish he would come over and try to play my PlayStation!
I'll wrap the controller around his neck.
That's why don't nobody like him.
Because he's stupid.
Can't get any girls.
Probably still pee the bed.
Every body's better than him at football.
Is that his car?
Yep, I see the dent on the driver side door.
Yes!
Thank-you.
Finally.

I did not appreciate my ride being late to pick me up at all; and my ex-girlfriend didn't either. You should always treat people the way you would like to be treated. You should respect your own time and the time of others. Our will wants us to have a positive image. One way to create a positive image is to always practice routines that show consideration to others and always be timely. You should discipline your body to always recognize important events; and discipline your body to always recognize important events; like birthdays and anniversaries of friends and family. To be timely is to be on time. One way to always be on time is to train your body to be ahead of time. Always be fifteen minutes early. By showing up fifteen minutes early to meetings and your place of employment you can learn a lot of valuable information. Fifteen minutes before the actual start time is usually when everyone is being their normal selves. Once the actual time hits; everyone plays their role. It's almost as if you have a V.I.P pass to go behind the scenes. When you show up fifteen minutes early, you might overhear your boss say he needs someone to volunteer to work at another facility for double their current salary. Or ask you a question about how to make the job more efficient. You can even use this time to ask questions. You can get better acquainted with your superiors and coworkers. You can find out about their favorite sports teams and hobbies. Once the actual time starts; it's as if the director says action because everyone starts playing their roles. Back to business as usual. Get in the habit of showing up fifteen minutes early. If you are picking someone up from work, let them look out the window and see their ride ahead of schedule. Use those fifteen minutes to relax or read a book or check emails. With today's technology, you can get a lot done in fifteen minutes. People will appreciate you being on time. They will see you as a dependable person, someone they can count on. You establish trust by being on time. People who are always in rush-rush, go-go mode have become slaves to the clock. They are always running behind time. Be disciplined and stay ahead of time. This will set you free. If you learn to control time you will never be a slave to the clock. Discipline your body to always recognize important events, birthdays' and anniversaries, of friends and family. Don't just rely on your brain to remember, write it down. One of the best habits I learned was to write thing down. Writing it down on paper helped me remember. I write down everything I need to do on my daily to do list. We all have had something that we needed to do only do draw a blank on what it actually is. That is the worse, when you can't remember what you remembered to do. To avoid being absent minded, make a daily to do list. Literally write down everything you need to do and make sure you do everything on your list. A typical daily to-do-list may look like this:

<u>Daily-to-do-list Wednesday June 23</u>
See if there is enough milk ☑
Call mother ☑
Find out what day the Bulls play the Heat ☑
See if cell phone can be upgraded ☑
Buy milk ☑
Leave son five dollars for field trip ☑
Turn porch light on ☑
Neighbors name is John ☑

Every night before I go to bed I make sure everything on my list is checked off. At the bottom of my list I wrote down my neighbors' name, John. This isn't a thing to do, but it is a thing to remember. I have always been bad with remembering people names. By me writing the name John and seeing it on paper helps me remember. I also have a digital special events calendar that I use to store birthday's and other special events. You should see the look on people faces that I'm barely acquainted with when I tell them happy birthday. The facial expression says, You really do like me. There actual words are, you remembered. You make people feel special when you remember the little things and our will loves to make people feel special. Start a daily To Do list and a reminder. They have many To Do lists and reminder apps that you can download and use. Make a good habit of writing every little thing down and reap all of the big rewards.

One thing you can't call me is forgetful. Thanks to my good habit of writing things down.

Why save what you can do today for tomorrow? Don't put it off for one more second. It will just build up and make tomorrows task seem impossible. I recommend you follow Larry the Cable Guy's famous saying and, "Get her done". The bedroom that you've been watching get messier and messier, go ahead and get her done. The car that you vowed to never drive dirty because it was your so called prized possession. Take the time to get her done. Don't allow the grass to grow another inch without getting her done. Your tools or cosmetics that you have been planning to organize; don't put it off another day, get her done! It's hard to get started because it looks like it will take forever. However, it never does. What you thought will take two hours to clean usually takes only a half an hour. Your body's mind will convince you to put off today's task for tomorrow and tomorrows task for next week. It will make excuses for you, such as, you need rest, it's going to take too long, it's too hard, or I can do it tomorrow. When you don't do the task that your will wants you to do, you feel guilty. You are quickly irritated easily annoyed and most times, you are unconscious as of why. As soon as you complete the task, it makes you feel better. You feel comfortable, less irritable less conscience stricken and you feel a lot more confident. That messy room that you always kept the door closed to, the blinds shut, and maneuvered around in the dark because you were ashamed of it. Now you got the door wide open, the sun shining in and you could care less about having unexpected guest. Your car that you finally got cleaned you are now proud to be seen in it. You now walk with your shoulders back and your head a little higher. From this day forward make a conscious decision to get her done. Most of the time whatever you are doing is not more important than what you willfully want to do. The phone and the TV can wait because ninety-nine percent of the time, they are of no importance to your will. Don't waste your time telling me or anyone else how you are going to sell all of your unwanted items in a rummage sale or how you are going to start spending more time with the spouse and kids. I may not be from the show me state but I will like for you to show me instead of tell me, by **"GETTING HER DONE!"**

Being scared or afraid is not an excuse to procrastinate. I have dealt with being afraid of failure most of my life. I can remember times when I was in grade school and I did not turn my homework in on time. Not because I didn't do it, but, because I was afraid I wasn't going to get an A or B. My teachers would always tell me a bad grade is better than no grade at all. I have once allowed my lights to get turned off in my home because I was afraid to get turned down for an extension. I didn't pay my utility bill on time and my family informed me that all I had to do was call and ask for an extension. By the time I worked up enough nerves to call, the representative told me it was too late because they already entered "proceed with termination" in the computer. If I would have called two days before hand, they would have allowed me an extension. It finally sunk in one day that a closed mouth will not get fed, I'm not always gone get the results that I want and I'm far from being perfect. If I strive to live up to perfection I am forever doomed of failure. There is absolutely no need to seek perfection. I don't worry about being out of my comfort zone. I just do my best and not worry about the rest. This book is a living testimony to that. You should always give your all. You can never be the best but you can do your best which is better than nothing at all. You can accomplish a lot if you will get off your butt and just do it.

SEX

❦

"How could something so wrong, feel so right? Can't worry about it tonight."

Those are the lyrics to the song, *4 Walls,* by the artist, Pretty Willie. Those lyrics express the artist's feelings that I'm very much familiar with. I've been there many times throughout my life. When you dissect the meaning behind those lyrics, you would find that they are saying, my heart knows this is wrong but it feels so good to my body that I'm just gonna give in and let my body enjoy this good feeling tonight and deal with the hearts 'will' later. After your body is done enjoying the sexual pleasures, your heart just feels terrible. The reason why you feel like this is because that wasn't your hearts will for you. You lose some of your morals, self-respect and self-esteem. I know some people are reading this and saying to themselves, why on earth would you feel like that. The reason why, is because some of us actually have good in our hearts. We know right from wrong we just don't always stay in control and impose our will over our bodies.

I remember a time when I was talking to this girl that I liked a lot. In a sexual attraction kind of way, not as a girl-

friend or wife. For the sake of this book, let's call her
Michelle. I spent a lot of time talking to Michelle on the
phone. We talked about everything. She even explained to
me that she did not want to have sex until she was married.
We both had two different objectives. Michelle wanted a
husband and I just wanted to have sex. Do you think I told
her that? Absolutely not! Michelle revealing that she only
wanted to have sex with her future husband should have
been enough to stop me in my tracks from pursuing her in a
sexual manner. But you know what, it didn't. You see, I
knew that her body might say something different. Have you
ever heard R. Kelly's song, *Bump and Grind*? He says, *"My
mind is telling me no but my body, my body is telling me
yeah."* Well what was her body saying? Would her body say
yeah? I had no idea but I surely wanted to find out. I was
confident that it would be easy to convince her body to give
in and say yes. All I had to do was give her body the pleasure it desired. My cocky arrogant attitude at this time in my
life made me feel that Beyoncé would want to sleep with me
if given the opportunity. I mean, I was God's gift to women,
they just didn't know it. One day after many attempts,
Michelle finally accepted one of my numerous invitations to
come to my house. *Now is my chance to woo her.*

I cleaned up the house really good. I lit candles in the
bedroom. Put on my favorite smell good at the time, Joop
for men. Please don't judge me, I was very young at the
time. I knew she did not like hard liquor at all. She only
liked wine coolers and wine. So I bought the best wine a
young man could buy, Boones Farm. I made sure I put it in
the freezer to stay chilled. I had a couple of frozen pizzas on
hand and a variety of movies. I wore some pajama pants and
a tank top to show off my athletic physique. I did push-ups
all the way up until the doorbell rang so my arms were big,
flowing with blood with huge veins popping out. After

Michelle and I ate some pizza, we lay down in bed and began spooning, while watching a love story with a buzz from the two dollar Boones Farm. I finally decided to make my move. I went in for a kiss and Michelle accepted my invitation. I began kissing and caressing her all over. As I was rounding second base and headed to third, I took off her shirt and unsnapped her bra. I could feel Michele start to resist. She tried to let a word roll off her tongue to let me know she didn't want to go any further, but, before she could I started sucking on her breast. The words she tried to get out turned into a long moan. It was her body's way of letting me know that it approved and enjoyed the pleasure I was giving it. I finally made my attempt to score by taking off her pants. Michelle immediately gained control of her body and let me know her will by verbalizing that she didn't want to do it. She firmly stated, "I'm saving myself for my husband, remember?"

My body felt like calling foul play but I didn't let her know it. Instead I assured Michelle that everything was all right when it actually wasn't. I had an agenda. I wanted to score so I did what was only right. I went back up to the plate and made my way back around to third. I remembered how Michelle responded last time. So this time I was a lot more passionate. She moaned crazily. I could feel her body burning with desire. She got caught in the heat of the moment and whispered in my ear, "I want you to make love to me."

Finally, her body was telling me yeah. There was just one problem. I completely forgot all about my body. I didn't get any protection. I couldn't believe that I forgot to get condoms. Having sex without a condom was against my will completely. I didn't want to have children by Michelle or put myself at greater risk of catching a S.T.D. or even AIDS. Unfortunately, sex without a condom was out of the question. I would just have to go get some condoms. My body immediately said "You can't stop and go get condoms while her body is burning for you because it won't be when you get back. As soon as you leave, her "will" is going to take over and remind her that she's waiting for marriage."

Once my body understood that leaving will more than likely ruin my chances of scoring, my will screamed out, "Oh no you don't! You don't play with me like that. I'm too excited to just throw it all away." My body went against my will and had sex with Michelle without a condom. Both of our bodies ended up rebelling against our "wills" and enjoyed indulging in the sexual pleasures. However, we both lost respect for ourselves in the process.

I can't tell you exactly how Michelle felt but I'm sure it was along the lines of feeling devalued, ashamed, disappointed or weak. I'm sure she felt small, because that's exactly how I was feeling. I was scared and haunted by that night for a long time. For about five months all I could worry about was her being pregnant. Every time I saw her I paid attention to her body to see if she was gaining weight. I watched to see if she was eating a lot or if she developed weird food cravings. I watched to see if she had used the restroom more frequently. I wanted to know if she was feeling nauseous and had she vomited. Not because I cared for her, but because I didn't want to have a baby. I had visions of my manhood tuning into a cauliflower. All the pictures I saw in health class of gonorrhea, syphilis and herpes were playing on the big screen in my head. A normal jock itch made me feel as if I had crabs. The thought of AIDS occurred in my head. I didn't want to go to the clinic because I would have been ashamed sitting in there. All of the attention would have embarrassed me. I finally got the results back letting me know that my manhood wasn't going to fall off and that I was H.I.V. negative. The feeling did not last long because shortly after, I found out that it could take five years to find out if you have H.I.V. What an emotional roller coaster I was going through. You would think that my body would give me some sort of support but it didn't. The body is extremely childish and selfish. I mean It thinks about self and self only. That one night of pleasure turned out to be years of torture.

Casual sex is one of the most horrific acts a person can commit to one's self. Casual sex is when you use each other for self-gratification or pleasure which turns yourself and others into objects. When someone is looked at as an object it dehumanizes them. They are seen as tools to be used instead of people. Have you ever paid attention to any of the euphemisms we use for having sex? To name a few, we say, hitting it, getting some, knocking boots, making whoopee, screwing, and the often used fucking. Do you notice any irony between screwing and fucking? You guessed it. You "screw" and "fuck" each other, literally. Casual sex destroys feelings and takes away the intimacy. When people are used as tools for having sex it goes against the best interest of others. The sex becomes driven by the desire for personal wholeness, selfishness and power. Sex is not supposed to be just a physical act, it's also mental and spiritual. In a committed relationship, sex is one of the greatest things that can happen between man and woman. Physically, mentally and spiritually sex is enjoyable and fulfilling in a committed relationship. Sex is the source for honor and pleasure. It helps build a better emotional and spiritual relationship with your partner. It's how you develop an exclusive intimacy with your lover. Sex creates the togetherness of two people. Sex is the act of love and grace: the donation of ones' self to your partner. It's an opened armed submission. The greatest beauty that comes from sex is the ability to give existence to life that will give existence to life. Man and women can do everything else on their own except procreate. We need each other. We were designed to complete each other. This completion only takes place when two people are committed to each other. The key word is committed. The only way to truly commit is by getting married. Sex and marriage go hand and hand. When you get married you enter into a union with your spouse: You deny everyone else and give your mind, body, and spirit solely to your spouse. Commitment without marriage means that your partner hasn't committed to all of you. More than likely, they have committed to your body and not your mind and spirit. You need them to commit to all three in order to have a healthy relationship. Sometimes a person will settle for the partner they are with at the moment while waiting on the one they truly want to arrive. It may seem like they are truly committed but the truth is, they are ready to jump ship at any moment, with only a moment's notice if any at all. If they are truly committed, they will seal the deal by putting a ring on it because they want you to have all of them in return for all of you. Not only did your partner tell you they want to live the rest of their life with you, they also signed documents to support it. I'm aware that a lot of marriages end in divorce, but many unmarried couples end in breakups. A lot of marriages end in divorce because the proper foundation to support the marriage was not laid. More than likely it was caused by premarital sex. This is why you should abstain from sexual intercourse before marriage. When you are in a non-sexual relationship that person gets to know you for you, not your sexuality. You develop better emotional and spiritual relationship with your partner. You can feel assured that your partner is with you because of your interest and personality. Showing trust to wait until you are married makes it a whole lot easier to trust faithfulness in marriage. When you practice abstinence it prevents sexual transmitted diseases. It gives you a better opportunity to focus and chase after your dreams. You don't have to worry about being compared to former lovers. It prevents abortions and unwanted children from being born without their mommies and daddies. It seems as if those who have kids they had no intentions on having, find it easier to run away from them.

Abstinence before marriage makes for a stronger marriage. I'm not an animal and you are not either. Naturally, a man's reproductive job is to plant seeds and a woman's job is to carry it. We were born this way and there is nothing we can do about it. Nevertheless, we can control it. Don't let your body lose you in the moment. Learn to own the moment by controlling it. The best way to stay out of a sticky situation is to not put yourself in one. Your body is vulnerable. It will give in to temptations without thinking twice about it. If you don't want to have sex, don't put the body in a situation where it can be sexually stimulated. The body becomes hard to control once it becomes stimulated sexually. The more stimulated the body is, the greater the difficulty becomes. The only thing the body begins to care about is sexual gratification. It takes a strong will to rise above sexual gratification and force the body to be more sensitive to what the *will* expects for the body. Put your body in a situation it can handle. Keep your body in alignment with your will by putting restrictions on your body. You have to limit what your body can and cannot do, because without restrictions you put your body at a greater risk of disobeying your will. In order to control your body, you have to learn to limit your risk. Don't cross third base if you don't want to cross home plate. I have witnessed women become victims to the moment because they put themselves in risky situations. Use Michelle and myself for example. Michelle should not have let me anywhere near second or third base if she did not want to have sex. She exposed her body to far too many risk. Once her body became sexually stimulated, the body took over and demanded sex. It is a lot easier to control the body on first base than it is third. Let's say the last time Michelle and I were alone together, we kissed and Michelle got sexually aroused. Michelle should probably avoid being alone with me kissing if she doesn't want it to lead to sex. Michelle can help control the outcome of situations by eliminating and adding different elements. Michelle could have eliminated being alone with me by adding friends to the equation. Instead of coming to my house alone she could have invited one of her friends to be present at all times. Michelle could have made sure that all of her dates with me were out in public to avoid any chance of crossing home plate. I know my pessimistic readers are saying Michelle could still end up having sex with her friends present and just because she goes out on a date with you in public doesn't mean you two can't have sex because people have sex in public all the time. I agree with you one hundred percent, and yes things can happen anywhere at any time. However, the goal we are trying to accomplish is limiting our risk. Michelle knows her body better than anyone. Michelle knows she is less likely to be seduced in front of her friend or in public. Through-out all of our lives there has been times where we could have prevented something from happening if we would have just limited our risk. Whether it be a seat belt to prevent fatality, or purchasing phone insurance to cover a lost or damaged phone. We could have prevented things from happening if we would have taken the time to limit our risk. Never put the body in a situation where it will more than likely go against your will. Keep in mind that you can contract H.I.V. wearing a condom but a condom reduces the chance of you catching H.I.V. drastically. Make sure you put the proper restrictions in place, because, if you play with fire you will get burned. Avoid your body from doing things detrimental to your will by limiting your risk.

I've been around some guys in my lifetime and it seems like sex is all they think about. A woman can't even walk past without them undressing her with their eyes. I know all they think about is sex because of some of the remarks that come out of their mouths. Like, "I know she a freak. She can probably go for hours. Her man isn't hitting that right," and my favorite, "I would love to butter that biscuit."

I have witnessed a couple of guys make and advance at women only to get turned down in the kind of way that will make Dwayne the Rock Johnson look small, put a smile on their face and tell me something along the lines of, she wants me, she was just letting me know that she likes it rough. Women are no better. Many female minds are stuck in the gutter also. I have heard some women say things like, "Ooh girl, he got some big feet! I would love to be wrapped in his big arms all night. The way he sucking on those chicken bones, I bet he can make my toes curl. One time, I asked a pretty young lady for her phone number only to hear her respond, "Are you sure you want my number because I am very fertile."

I'm pretty sure you have heard or said worse in your lifetime. Our thoughts can be very poisonous to our bodies if we don't learn to control them. Have you ever thought about what genuinely good people think about all day? Take a second and try to imagine what Mother Teresa or Martin Luther King Jr or John Paul II, thought about all day. Now try to imagine what pedophiles, rapist and perverts think about all day. What category did you find yourself in?

Even if you just have the thoughts in your head, it still doesn't make it okay. How would you feel if one of your friends had sex with your partner from time to time but only in their head? Will you be okay with that? How many people will be all right with you if they know that you undress them with your eyes? I'm sure they will feel that you have violated them and that you have crossed the line. When those unfruitful thoughts creep into your mind, you must not pay them any attention.

You are less likely to get divorced when you take the time to grow a stronger bond with your partner that doesn't involve sex. The world we live in today is constantly putting pressure on us to have multiple sex partners and sex before marriage. This is the same world that tells us that sex is safe as long as you use a condom. Not to mention all of the spiritual and emotional baggage that comes along with it. Yes, sex with condom is safer but not safe. There are only two forms of safe sex and that is no sex at all, and married sex.

Once you are married, feel free to enjoy the gift of sex, but do not use sex as a weapon. Many married couples start out with a healthy sex life but overtime it becomes lost. If I were to poll couples around the world, most will say that coming into the relationship with their partner, they wanted to please their partner sexually. Most will say they had a healthy sex life in the beginning but over time, the healthy sex life is lost due to couples not following their "will". They no longer try to please their partner sexually. Their body that they once gave to their partner freely, they now give under conditions: If you buy me the car I want, if you skip bowling night with your friends, or if you take me on a cruise. It may not be said directly but it is communicated in some way or form indirectly. One of the ways your will shows your partner unconditional love is by yielding authority of your body to your partner. Therefore, when you commit to a relationship you submit your body to your lover. A wife submits her body to her husband and a husband submits his body to his wife. A couple should not deprive each other of sex unless there is a mutual agreement, a time of fasting, an illness or the women is going through her menstrual cycle. Your body is priceless, so don't ever put a price on it. Don't let a bouquet of roses be the reason you have sex. Don't let a diamond ring or seven-day cruise be the reason you have sex either. Have sex because that's one of the many ways that you express your love to your spouse. Women tend to give sex to get love and men tend to give love to get sex. By imposing your will, you can have a healthier relationship with your spouse. It can be full of amazing sex. My advice is, make love to your partner without the conditions.

Spirit

I spent most of my life uncomfortable about many of the decisions I made throughout my life. I thought I knew it all only to find out that I knew nothing. I thought I could do it all on my own only to find out that I needed help. I thought my way was the right way only to find out that it was wrong. It wasn't until I fell to my lowest point, that I realized I had life all wrong. I was not living out my purpose in life. I was created for a purpose but what was it? If I wanted to find my purpose I knew I had to go to the ruler of the universe, the supreme being, the one whom created me. I began looking for God. I searched every religious book I could get my hands on and asked everyone who would give me an answer about God. In my search, I found a lot of false gods and a lot of religion. I never did find God, he actually found me. He found me in my mess and lifted me out of it. He led me to the Bible, which I was very familiar with and have read many times throughout my life. I had actually turned away from the Bible because of the way religions misrepresented it. I had no faith nor trust in the Bible. It had become just another word I heard. However, this time I studied Gods word and meditated on it daily. I began speaking to God and he began speaking to me. Through His word, He showed how loving merciful and gracious He is versus how legalistic, unforgiving and punishing the religious people made Him out to be. God let me know that I can be forgiven for all of my sins if I would simply ask and accept His Son, Jesus Christ as my Lord and Savior. I did and felt a peace I never felt before and the greatest joy came over me. Redeemed is how I felt. God let me know that He wants me to live with Him so He can love on me forever. God showed me that my purpose in life was to do good works through His Son, Christ Jesus. You see, God had given me his spirit, and I allowed it to be lord of my life. Contrary to the title of this book, my will is actually His will. I let God impose his perfect will over my life. With that in mind, please note. I am not a doctor, psychiatrist, social worker, counselor, pastor, teacher or anything of the sort. In fact, I am a convict, and a sinner who has broken all of Gods commandments. Getting saved did not make me perfect either, but what it did do was save my life and the same can happen to you. I hope you don't mind but I would like to end this book in prayer.

Heavenly Father, I thank You for allowing me to be Your son and using me to reach out to Your children. I ask You to open the minds, eyes and hearts of those who don't believe or are unsure of who You really are. Call on them Father. Show them that You are the one and only, living, loving and merciful God. Give them a thirst and hunger for Your word. Bring them to confess their sins and accept Your Son, Jesus Christ as their lord and savior. I ask of You to transform their lives and let them live in the image that You created them in. Yet not my will, Your will.

Amen

CITATIONS

꞊ೞ꞊

[a] 1 Rom. 7: 15, NIV

[b] Rom. 7: 24, NIV

[c] Matt. 5: 37, NIV

[d] Matt. 5: 36, NIV

[e] 1 Cor. 3: 4 - 8, NIV

[f] Luke 12: 15, NIV

www.ingramcontent.com/pod-product-compliance
Lightning Source LLC
Chambersburg PA
CBHW052012090426
42741CB00008B/1657